Chemistry
Science Fair Projects
Using Inorganic Stuff

Library of Congress Cataloging-in-Publication Data

Gardner, Robert, 1929–
    Chemistry science fair projects using inorganic stuff, revised and expanded using the scientific method / by Robert Gardner.
        p. cm. — (Chemistry science projects using the scientific method)
    Summary: "Explains how to use the scientific method to conduct several inorganic chemistry experiments. Includes ideas for science fair projects"—Provided by publisher.
    Includes bibliographical references and index.
    ISBN-13: 978-0-7660-3413-6
    ISBN-10: 0-7660-3413-5
    1. Chemistry—Experiments—Juvenile literature. 2. Science projects—Juvenile literature. I. Title.
    QD38.G354 2010
    540.78 dc22
                        2008046505

Printed in the United States of America

092009 Lake Book Manufacturing, Inc., Melrose Park, IL

10 9 8 7 6 5 4 3 2 1

To Our Readers: We have done our best to make sure all Internet Addresses in this book were active and appropriate when we went to press. However, the author and the publisher have no control over and assume no liability for the material available on those Internet sites or on other Web sites they may link to. Any comments or suggestions can be sent by e-mail to comments@enslow.com or to the address on the back cover.

♻ Enslow Publishers, Inc. is committed to printing our books on recycled paper. The paper in every book contains between 10% to 30% post-consumer waste (PCW). The cover board on the outside of each book contains 100% PCW. Our goal is to do our part to help young people and the environment too!

Illustration Credits: Tom LaBaff and Stephanie LaBaff

Editorial Revision: Lily Book Productions

Design: Oxygen Design

Photo Credits: Jan Rihak/iStockphoto.com, p.6; Jim Jurica/iStockphoto.com, p. 134; Simon Podgorsek/iStockphoto.com, p. 3; Shutterstock, pp. 26, 84, 106; *Traité élémentaire de chimie (Elementary Treatise on Chemistry)*, by Antoine Lavoisier, p. 68; Wikimedia Commons, 75, 83.

Cover Photos: Shutterstock

Revised edition of *Chemistry Science Fair Projects Using Acids, Bases, Metals, Salts, and Inorganic Stuff.* Copyright © 2004.

Chemistry Science Fair Projects Using Inorganic Stuff

Revised and Expanded
Using the Scientific Method

Robert Gardner

 Enslow Publishers, Inc.
40 Industrial Road
Box 398
Berkeley Heights, NJ 07922
USA
http://www.enslow.com

Contents

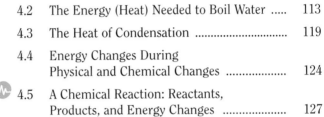
Indicates activities appropriate for science fair projects.

INTRODUCTION

Chemistry Experiments and Projects Using the Scientific Method

Chemistry is the part of science that deals with what materials are made of and how they combine with one another. Chemists know how to keep your new bike from rusting, why pizzas are delivered in insulated bags, and what to use to remove stains from your clothing. They divide their work into two types: the study of materials that are organic and those that are not. Organic chemistry deals with compounds containing carbon, many of which are found in living things, such as plants and animals. Inorganic chemistry studies all the other substances, such as water, air, metals, salts, and many more.

This book will focus on projects and experiments related to inorganic chemistry. Another book in this series covers organic chemistry.

◀ These piles of rock salt (halite), an inorganic substance made up mostly of sodium chloride, were mined from the largest salt flat in the world: Salar de Uyuni, Bolivia.

Experiments and Projects

This book contains lots of fun experiments about inorganic chemistry. You will also be given suggestions for independent investigations that you can do yourself. Many of the experiments are followed by a section called Science Project Ideas. This section contains great ideas for your own science fair projects.

The experiments are all easy to do and safe to carry out when the instructions are followed as given. Consult with your school science teacher or some **other responsible adult** to obtain approval before starting any experiments of your own.

Most of the materials you will need to carry out the projects and experiments described in this book can be found in your home. Several of the experiments may require items that you

How Scientists Search for Answers

When scientists have a question to answer, they start by researching. They read scientific literature and consult online science databases that are maintained by universities, research centers, or the government. There, they can study abstracts—summaries of reports—by scientists who have conducted experiments or done similar research in the field.

In this way, they find out whether other scientists have examined the same question or have tried to answer it by doing an experiment. Careful research will tell what kind of experiments, if any, have been done to try to answer the question.

Scientists don't want to repeat experiments that have known and accepted outcomes. Also, they want to avoid can buy from a supermarket, a hobby or toy shop, a hardware store, or one of the science-supply companies listed in the appendix. Some of the experiments in Chapters 2, 3, and 4 require special equipment, like a Bunsen burner. As you begin to use this book, show it to one of the science teachers in your school. Perhaps the teacher will allow you and some of your friends to use the school's equipment. At times, you will need a partner to help you. It would be best if you work with friends or adults who enjoy experimenting as much as you do. In that way you will both enjoy what you are doing.

repeating any mistakes others may have made while doing similar experiments. If no one else has done scientific work that answers the question, scientists then do further research on how best to do the experiment. While researching for the experiment, the scientist tries to guess—or predict—the possible results. This prediction is called a hypothesis.

The scientist hopes that a well-researched and carefully planned experiment will prove the hypothesis to be true. At times, however, the results of even the best-planned experiment can be far different from what the scientist expected. Yet even if the results indicate the hypothesis was not true, this does not mean the experiment was a failure. In fact, unexpected results can provide valuable information that leads to a different answer or to another, even better, experiment.

Using the Scientific Method in Experiments and Projects

The Scientific Method

A scientific experiment starts when someone wonders what would happen if certain conditions were set up and tested by following a specific process. For example, in an experiment testing the rate (speed) of a chemical reaction, we can ask the question: Which would react faster, a substance with a larger surface area or an identical substance with a smaller surface area? A guess about what would happen is your hypothesis, and some possible hypotheses might be:

✓ The substance (reactant) with the larger surface area will be slower to react.

✓ The substance with the smaller surface area will react faster.

✓ The reaction rate will be the same.

Let's say your hypothesis is that the substance with more surface area would have a slower rate of reaction.

For a start, we have to know that a scientific experiment has only two variables—that is, only two things that can change. For this experiment, one variable is the rate of the chemical reactions and the other is the different surface areas of the reactants. The reactant with the larger surface area is a solid seltzer tablet, and the other is a crushed seltzer tablet.

The surface areas of the reactants are allowed to be different. Everything else, however, must be the same: the amount of seltzer, the amounts of water in which the reactants are placed, and the water temperatures. If anything besides the surface area were different, it would not be possible to tell what had affected the rates of reaction.

Now, if there is no difference in reaction rates when the experiment is carried out, this would not mean the experiment is a failure. Even if your hypothesis—that the reactant with more surface area would react more slowly—turns out to be false, all your results, positive or negative, provide important information. And the results can lead to further ideas that can be explored.

Scientists may develop logical explanations for the results of their experiments. These explanations, or theories, must be tested by more experiments. If the resulting data from experiments provide compelling support for a theory, the theory could be accepted by the world of science. But scientists are careful about accepting new theories. If any of the experimental results contradict a theory, then the theory must be discarded, altered, or retested. That is the scientific method.

Basic Steps in the Scientific Method

The best experiments and science projects usually follow the scientific method's basic steps:

✓ Ask questions about what would happen if certain conditions or events were set up and tested in an experiment.

✓ Do background research to investigate the subject of your question.

✓ Construct a hypothesis—an answer to your question—that you can then test and investigate with an experiment.

✓ Design and conduct an experiment to test your hypothesis.

✓ Keep records, collecting data, and then analyze what you've recorded.

✓ Draw a conclusion based on the experiment and the data you've recorded.

✓ Write a report about your results.

Your Hypothesis

Many experiments and science projects begin by asking whether something can be done or how it can be done. In this book's experiment, "Influencing the Rate of a Reaction," the question is, "Do external factors affect the speed of a chemical reaction?"

The educated guess—the hypothesis—that answers the question is, "Yes. Factors that affect chemical reactions include changes in temperature, the surface area being tested, and the concentration of the reactants."

How do you test this hypothesis? First you should study how chemical reactions take place and learn the difference between a chemical reaction and a physical reaction. What sort of factors—heat, other chemicals added, a substance's solubility in water—are known to cause or influence chemical reactions. Do some background research into whether these factors could cause a reaction in the substances with which you wish to experiment.

You also should find out what methods, chemicals, and equipment are needed to design an experiment that will test your hypothesis. By using the right tools and materials—in this case seltzer tablets, hot and cold water, clear plastic cups, and a watch or clock for a timer—you can study and record the rates of chemical reactions when different external factors are applied.

Remember: To give your experiment or project every chance of success, prepare a hypothesis that is clear and brief. The simpler the hypothesis, the better it is.

Designing the Experiment

Your experiment will be structured to investigate whether the hypothesis is true or false. The experiment is intended to test the hypothesis, but not necessarily to prove that the hypothesis is right.

The results of a well-designed experiment are more valuable than the results of an experiment that is intentionally designed to give the answer you want. The conditions you set up in your experiment must be a fair test of your hypothesis. For example, in the rates of chemical change experiment, you should follow the instructions carefully when measuring out and heating water and when controlling and measuring the amount of gas caused by the reaction.

Remember: Scientists around the world always use metric measurements in their experiments and projects, and so should you. Use metric liquid and dry measures and a Celsius thermometer.

Pay close attention to what happens when different experimental conditions are set up, when different concentrations of a substance are used, or when temperatures are varied. By carefully carrying out your experiment, you'll discover use-ful information that can be recorded as data (observations).

It's most important that the experiment's procedures and results are as accurate as possible. Design the experiment for observable, measurable results. And keep it simple, because the more complicated your experiment is, the more chance you have for error.

Also, if you have friends helping you with an experiment or project, make sure from the start that they will take their tasks seriously.

Recording Data

Your hypothesis, procedure, data, and conclusions should be recorded immediately as you experiment, but don't keep it on loose scraps of paper. Record your data in a notebook or log-book—one you use just for experiments. Your notebook should be bound so that you have a permanent record. The laboratory notebook is an essential part of all academic and scientific research.

Make sure to include the date, experiment number, and a brief description of how you collected the data. Write clearly.

If you have to cross something out, do it with just a single line, then rewrite the correct information.

Repeat your experiment several times to be sure your results are consistent and your data are trustworthy. Don't try to interpret data as you go along. It's better first to record results accurately, then study them later.

You might even find that you want to replace your experiment's original question with a new one. For example, the question, "Do external factors affect the speed of a chemical reaction?" brings up another question: "Why do catalysts *cause* a chemical reaction—a change in the reactants—but they *don't change chemically* themselves?"

Writing the Science Fair Report

Communicate the results of your experiment by writing a clear report. Even the most successful experiment loses its value if the scientist cannot clearly tell what happened. Your report should describe how the experiment was designed and conducted and should state its precise results.

Following are the parts of a science fair report, in the order they should appear:

• Title Page

The title of your experiment should be centered and near the top of the page. Your teacher will tell you what other information is needed, such as your name, your grade, and the name of your science teacher.

• Table of Contents

On the report's second page, list the remaining parts of the report and their page numbers.

• Abstract

Give a brief overview of your experiment. In just a few sentences, tell the purpose of the experiment, what you did, and what you found out. Always write in plain, clear language.

• Introduction

State your hypothesis and explain how you came up with it. Discuss your experiment's main question and how your research led to the hypothesis. Tell what you hoped to achieve when you started the experiment.

• Experiment and Data

This is a detailed step-by-step explanation of how you organized and carried out the experiment. Explain what methods you followed and what materials and equipment you used.

State when the experiment was done (the date and perhaps the time of day) and under what conditions (in a laboratory, outside on a windy day, in cold or warm weather, etc.). Tell who was involved and what part they played in the experiment. Include clearly labeled graphs and tables of data from the experiment as well as any photographs or drawings that help illustrate your work. Anyone who reads your report should be able to repeat the experiment just the way you did it. (Repeating an experiment is a good way to test whether the original results were obtained correctly.)

• Discussion

Explain your results and conclusions, perhaps comparing them with published scientific data you first read about in your research. Consider how the experiment's results relate to your hypothesis. Ask yourself: Do my results support or contradict my hypothesis? Then analyze the answer.

Would you do anything differently if you did this experiment again? State what you've learned as a result of the experiment. Analyze how your tools and equipment did their tasks, and how well you and others used those tools. If you think the experiment could be designed a better way or if you have another hypothesis that might be tested, then include this in your discussion.

• Conclusion

Make a brief summary of your experiment's results. Include only information and data already stated in the report, and be sure not to bring in any new information.

• Acknowledgments

Give credit to everyone who helped you with the experiment. State the names of these individuals and briefly explain who they are and how they assisted you.

• References / Bibliography

List any books, magazines, journals, articles, Web sites, scientific databases, and interviews that were important to your research for the experiment.

Science Fairs

Science fair judges tend to reward creative thought and imagination. It's difficult to be creative or imaginative unless you're really interested in your project. So, be sure to choose a subject that appeals to you. And before you jump into a project, consider your own talents and the cost of the materials you'll need.

Remember, judges at science fairs don't reward projects or experiments that are simply copied from a book. For example, a diagram or model of an atom or molecule wouldn't impress most judges. However, designing an experiment to find out how a chemical reaction is affected by temperature or pressure would attract their attention.

If you decide to use a project from this book for a science fair, you should find ways to modify or extend it. This shouldn't be difficult, because you'll probably discover that, as you do these projects, new ideas for experiments will come to mind. These experiments could make excellent science fair projects, particularly because the ideas are your own and are interesting to you.

If you decide to enter a science fair and have never done so before, you should read some of the books listed in the Further Reading section and visit the Internet sites. The books and sites with titles that refer to science fairs will provide plenty of helpful hints and information that will help you avoid the pitfalls that sometimes plague first-time entrants.

You'll learn how to prepare appealing reports that include charts and graphs, how to set up and display your work, how to present your project, and how to relate to judges and visitors.

Following are some suggestions to consider.

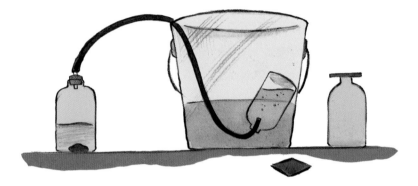

Some Tips for Success at a Science Fair

Science teachers and science fair judges have many different opinions on what makes a good science fair project or experiment. Here are the most important elements:

Originality of Concept is one of the most important things judges consider. Some judges believe that the best science fair projects answer a question that is not found in a science textbook.

Scientific Content is another main area of evaluation. How was science applied in the procedure? Are there sufficient data? Did you stick to your intended procedure and keep good records?

Thoroughness is next in importance. Was the experiment repeated as often as needed to test your hypothesis? Is your notebook complete, and are the data accurate? Does your research bibliography show you did enough library work?

Clarity in how you present your exhibit shows you had a good understanding of the subject you worked on. It is important that your exhibit clearly presents the results of your work.

Effective Process: Judges recognize that how skillfully you carry out a science fair project is usually more important than its results. A well-done project gives students the best understanding of what scientists actually do day-to-day.

Other points to consider when preparing for your science fair:

The Abstract: Write up a brief explanation of your project and make copies for visitors or judges who want to read it.

Knowledge: Be ready to answer questions from visitors and judges confidently. Know what is in your notebook and make some notes on index cards to remind you of important points.

Practice: Before the science fair begins, prepare a list of several questions you think you might be asked. Think about the answers and about how your display can help to support them. Have a friend or parent ask you questions and answer them out loud. Knowing your work thoroughly helps you feel more confident when you're asked about it.

Appearance: Dress and act in a way that shows you take your project seriously. Visitors and judges should get the impression that you're interested in the project and take pride in answering their questions about it.

Remember: Don't block your exhibit. Stand to the side when someone is looking at it.

Projects about chemistry have special needs with respect to displays. You cannot show the chemical changes as they take place. Instead, photograph or draw them. Many chemical changes are colorful, so use color to make pictures more striking. Show the materials used at the start of the reaction and those produced at the end of the reaction by enclosing them in containers, such as sealed petri dishes or plastic bags that you mount on a display. Photograph or draw any special laboratory tools and the laboratory apparatus you set up. Be inventive about different ways of showing what took place.

Safety First

Experimenting with chemicals can be dangerous unless certain precautions are taken. It is your responsibility to use all the chemicals only as directed in this book. The precautions necessary to prevent accidents and to make the experiments safe and enjoyable are easy to follow.

✔ Consideration must always be given to safety. Therefore, it's essential that **all investigations and science fair projects be approved by a responsible adult.** Where warranted, the experimentation should take place **under adult supervision.** If there are any questions about safety, **the adult** should be sure to obtain the approval of a science teacher before allowing the experiments.

✔ Whenever doing chemistry experiments, it's a good idea to wear goggles (safety glasses). All chemists wear goggles when working in the laboratory. Goggles can be purchased in hardware or dollar stores. Most of the substances are not dangerous, but they might sting your eyes if they splatter.

✔ Read all instructions carefully before proceeding with a project. If you have questions, check with your supervisor before going any further.

✔ Never taste any materials listed in this book unless specifically directed to do so. Never put your fingers to your mouth while working on an experiment.

✔ Always wash your hands with warm water and soap after an experiment. Also, wash the surfaces on which you have carried out the experiment.

✔ Never use a mercury thermometer because exposure to mercury is dangerous; use mercury-free alternatives, such as thermometers containing alcohol.

✔ When using certain solvents, adequate ventilation is necessary, such as an exhaust fan or an open window.

✔ Some solvents are flammable and should not be used near a flame.

✔ Wear plastic gloves when handling chemicals. The thin disposable gloves that may be used on either hand are often sold in packs of one hundred in dollar stores or hardware stores and are very convenient for this purpose.

✔ Some chemicals should not be flushed down the sink or thrown into the garbage. Instructions will be given for disposal of any such materials used in an experiment.

✔ Maintain a serious attitude while conducting experiments. Fooling around can be dangerous to you and to others.

✔ Never let water droplets come in contact with a hot light bulb.

✔ Never experiment with household electricity except under the supervision of a **knowledgeable adult**.

✔ It's a good idea to wear an apron and to work on surfaces that can resist water damage. Covering a surface with newspapers or plastic sheeting will help to protect it.

✔ You should use purified water for experiments unless otherwise stated. Distilled or deionized water sold at the supermarket may be used for this purpose. Natural water from a spring or other source may be safe to drink, but is not considered pure because it contains dissolved solids.

And now, on to the experiments!

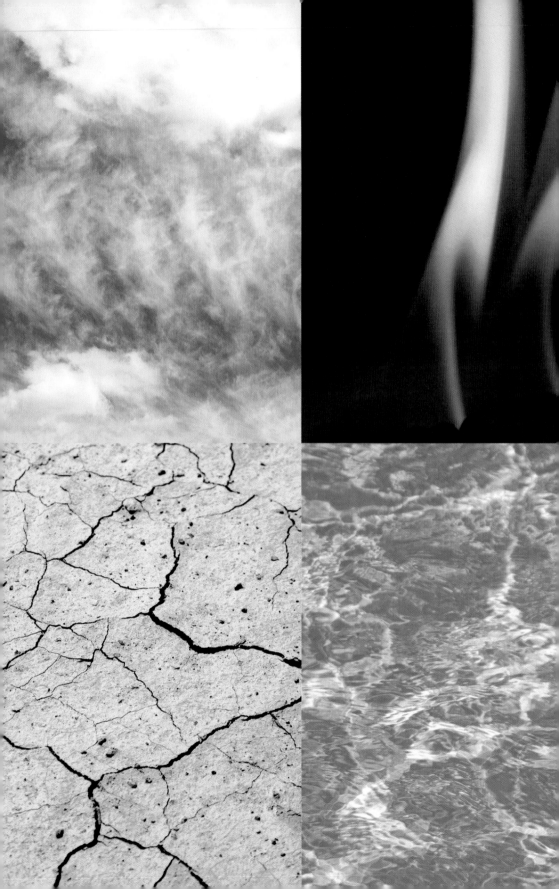

CHAPTER 1

Identifying Substances

Early Greek philosophers believed that all matter was made up of four basic elements–earth, air, fire, and water. These elements had the effect of dryness, coldness, hotness, and wetness on other objects. The amount of each element was different in different types of objects.

The idea that any kind of matter consisted of a particular combination of earth, air, fire, and water led to alchemy—the notion that matter could be transmuted (changed). The alchemists (the people who practiced alchemy) believed they could transmute matter from one form to another. They tried to convert less valuable metals, such as lead, into gold, which they regarded as

◀ Alchemists and philosophers in ancient times believed matter was made up of earth, air, fire, and water.

the "perfect" form of matter. Undoubtedly, the value attached to this metal inspired their research.

Although they never succeeded, their work led to many useful chemistry techniques, such as distillation and filtering (ways of purifying liquids) and crystal growing. Modern chemists still use these techniques. Alchemists discovered a number of substances that we recognize as true elements— phosphorus, antimony, bismuth, and zinc, among others. They identified many compounds such as salts, acids, bases, and alcohols.

Practical Alchemy

By the seventeenth century, the alchemists' failure to transmute other substances into gold led many to abandon the search. However, some alchemists went on using practical techniques that led to a better understanding of matter. These scientists realized that most samples of matter, such as rocks, dirt, and seawater, are mixtures. Mixtures, they learned, can be separated into substances whose characteristic properties (density, solubility, boiling temperature, etc.) are unchanging. They discovered that these pure substances were of two kinds: elements and compounds. Elements were seen as substances that could not be decomposed into simpler substances by any chemical means. Compounds, on the other hand, were substances that could be broken down into elements. Our modern view of matter is basically the same.

Most matter exists in mixtures. To find out what substances are in a particular mixture, we must first separate the mixture into its components. Then we have to identify the substances we separated. How can we do that?

The elements and compounds extracted from a mixture are identified by their properties. These properties, which distinguish one substance from another, include its state (solid, liquid, or gas), density, boiling and freezing temperatures, solubility in water and other liquids, conductivity (of heat and electricity), color of light emitted when heated, and other characteristic properties.

EXPERIMENT 1.1

Separating the Components of a Mixture

Question:

How can a mixture of solids be separated into its components?

Hypothesis:

Each component of any mixture of solids usually has characteristics that can be used to separate it from the others.

Materials:

- **an adult**
- plastic cup
- teaspoon
- sawdust
- salt
- sand
- iron filings (if available) or steel wool (without soap) cut into small pieces with scissors
- paper
- magnet
- drinking glass
- water
- Pyrex beaker or small baking dish
- oven mitt
- oven
- funnel
- filter paper or white coffee filter
- ring and ring stand or some other way of supporting a funnel

Procedure:

1. In a plastic cup, mix together a teaspoonful of each of the following: sawdust, salt, sand, and iron or steel wool filings.

2. Spread the solids out into a thin layer on a sheet of paper. Pass a magnet over the solids. Is any component of the mixture attracted to the magnet? If it is, remove that solid from the mixture and place it on a separate piece of paper.

3. Pour the remaining mixture into a drinking glass, add some water and stir. Do any components of the mixture dissolve in the water? Do any of the components float on the surface of the water? Which component can you easily separate at this stage? How will you do it?

4. Remove that component from the mixture and place it on a piece of paper to dry.

5. Can you separate the remaining components by pouring off the liquid? You might try that by pouring the liquid into a Pyrex beaker or a small baking dish. Spread the solid out on a piece of paper where it can dry.

6. **Ask an adult** to place the container that holds the liquid in a warm (120°F) oven where the liquid can evaporate. After the water has evaporated, **ask an adult** to use an oven mitt and remove the beaker or dish from the oven. What do you find in the beaker or dish?

7. Examine the solid after it has dried. Is there any evidence of salt crystals among the grains of sand? If there is, pour the sand into a glass or beaker, add water, and stir to dissolve the salt.

8. Use a ring and a ring stand, borrowed from a science teacher, or some other means to support a funnel, such as a board with a hole in it. Line the funnel with a piece of filter paper and pour the liquid and sand

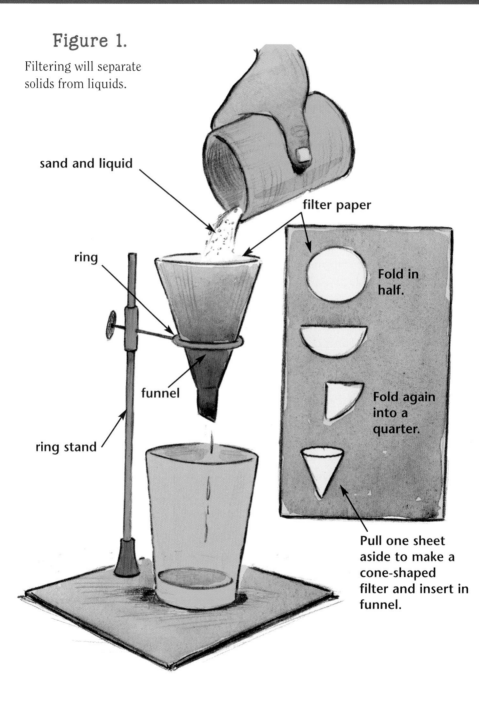

Figure 1.

Filtering will separate solids from liquids.

sand and liquid

filter paper

ring

Fold in half.

funnel

Fold again into a quarter.

ring stand

Pull one sheet aside to make a cone-shaped filter and insert in funnel.

into it, as shown in Figure 1. (If you don't have the round filter paper used in chemistry courses, you can use a white coffee filter.)

9. Collect the liquid that passes through the filter paper in a glass or beaker. Rinse the sand that remains on the paper by pouring water over it. Once the liquid has passed through the filter, evaporate the liquid and dry the sand as before.

Results and Conclusions

When the liquid has evaporated and the sand has dried, examine the sand and the beaker or glass again. Have you finally separated all the components of the original mixture?

Consider how the various physical characteristics of sawdust, salt, sand, and iron or steel wool filings allowed you to separate them from the original mixture. Why was it appropriate to start with the magnet? Analyze the results of each of the other steps:

a) adding water caused one component to float

b) boiling off the water revealed the remaining two components

c) adding more water made it possible to filter the mixture to capture one of these components.

The unique characteristics of each component—especially with regard to being mixed with water—made it possible to separate them from one another.

 Science Project Ideas

- About 3.5 percent of seawater is salt. How can drinking water be obtained from seawater? If you can obtain some seawater, design an experiment to separate the water from the salt. Then, **under adult supervision,** carry out the experiment.

- In some desert countries, people obtain drinking water from seawater. How do they do this? Why is it expensive to do?

- How might you go about separating two salts, such as sodium chloride and potassium nitrate, that are both soluble in water?

EXPERIMENT 1.2

Separating by Chromatography

Question:

Are there ways to separate color components of ink or food coloring?

Hypothesis:

Paper chromatography can separate pigments in ink or food coloring.

Materials:

- black ink
- red, green, blue, and yellow food coloring
- water
- filter papers or white coffee filters or blotter paper
- funnel

- scissors
- ruler
- colored marking pens
- blue and black ink pens
- toothpicks
- tape
- wide, shallow dish

You can use paper chromatography to try to separate the pigments in ink and food coloring. These substances often contain more than one pigment. Can you separate the colored substances by filtering?

Procedure:

1. To find out, add a few drops of black ink and a few drops each of red, green, blue, and yellow food coloring to about 5 mL of water.

2. Then fold a piece of filter paper or a coffee filter as was shown in Figure 1. Place the filter in a funnel.

3. Pour the mixture of water, ink, and food coloring onto it. Is the liquid that comes through the filter paper clear or is it still colored? What happens to the color on the filter after an hour or two?

4. You may have noticed that the colored pigments on the filter began to separate into different colors. To separate the colors that may be in ink and food coloring, cut some strips 2 cm × 15 cm (1 in × 6 in) from white coffee filters, filter paper, or white blotter paper.

5. Near the bottom of one strip, paint a stripe using one of your colored samples (food coloring or ink). A toothpick can be used to paint the stripes of food coloring.

6. Prepare separate strips for each sample. Use different colored marking pens and blue and black ink pens to "paint" on some colored inks.

7. When the strips are dry, use tape to hang them from a kitchen cupboard, as shown in Figure 2. The bottom ends of the strips should just touch the water in a wide, shallow dish.

Results and Conclusions

What happens as water climbs the paper? Do any of the colors separate into different pigments? Would this method work if the pigments were not soluble in water? Can you put the pigments back together again?

Figure 2.

Paper chromatography is sometimes used to separate substances in a mixture.

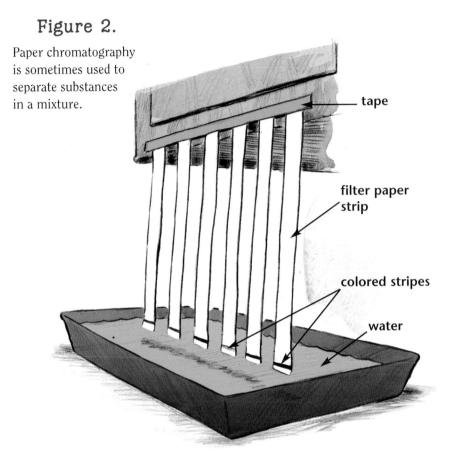

tape

filter paper strip

colored stripes

water

Science Project Idea

- Investigate the different types of chromatography, such as column, thin layer, high-pressure liquid, and gas. How does each of these various forms of chromatography separate the components of a mixture? How do forensic scientists use chromatography to help solve crimes?

EXPERIMENT 1.3

Using Density to Identify Liquids

Question:

What is an important characteristic of liquids that helps identify and distinguish them?

Hypothesis:

The density of a liquid—its weight per volume—can often be used to help identify it.

Materials:

- 100-mL graduated cylinder
- a balance
- water
- eyedropper (optional)
- isopropyl rubbing alcohol (isopropanol)
- cooking oil
- drinking glass
- pencil and paper
- 4 aluminum cans of cola: regular cola, which contains caffeine and sugar; decaffeinated cola with sugar; decaffeinated diet cola (no sugar); and diet cola with caffeine
- pail of water

Procedure:

1. Weigh a 100-mL graduated cylinder on a balance. Record the weight and then fill the cylinder to the 100-mL line with water. Because water adheres to the surface of the cylinder, the top of the water curves down. This concave surface is called a meniscus. To accurately measure the volume, the bottom of the meniscus should just touch the 100-mL line, as shown in Figure 3a.

2. If necessary, use an eyedropper to add or remove a small amount of water. Once you have exactly 100 mL of water, reweigh the cylinder and water. How can you find the weight of the water alone?

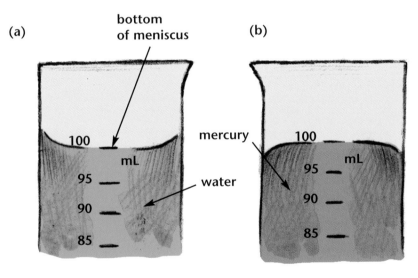

Figure 3.

a) Because water sticks (adheres) to glass or plastic, you should read the volume of water from the bottom of its meniscus.

b) Some substances, such as mercury, do not adhere to glass. Their surface in a glass vessel is convex rather than concave.

Results and Conclusions

Knowing the weight and volume of the water, you can easily calculate the density of water by dividing the weight by the volume.

$$\text{Density} = \frac{\text{Weight, g}}{\text{Volume, mL}}$$

How many grams of water are contained in each milliliter? Express the density of water as grams per milliliter (g/mL). Since a milliliter and a cubic centimeter (cm^3) have the same volume, how else might you express the density of water? Does the density you calculated agree closely with the value for water found in Table 1?

Next, find the density of isopropyl alcohol, also known as isopropanol or rubbing alcohol. Does the density of the rubbing alcohol correspond to any of the liquids found in Table 1?

You might have expected the liquid would have the same density as isopropanol. However, if you read the finer print, you will see that rubbing alcohol is only 70 percent isopropanol. If we assume that the other 30 percent is water, we can make a good estimate of the liquid's density. (When alcohol and water are mixed, the volume of the mixture is slightly less than the sum of the two volumes when separated.)

Suppose we have 100 mL of rubbing alcohol made by mixing 70 mL of isopropanol with 30 mL of water. The water will weigh 30 g. Since each milliliter of the alcohol weighs 0.79 grams, the weight of 70 mL will be:

$$70 \text{ mL} \times 0.79 \text{ g/mL} = 55.3 \text{ g}$$

The total weight will be 85.3 g (30 g + 55.3 g). Hence, the estimated density would be:

$$85.3 \text{ g} \div 100 \text{ mL} = 0.853 \text{ g/mL}$$

How does this value compare with the value that you found for the density of rubbing alcohol?

Table 1.
Densities of Some Liquids, Solids, and Gases

Substance	Density (g/mL or g/cm³)	Substance	Density (g/cm³)
Liquids		**Solids**	
Acetone	0.79	Aluminum	2.7
Ethanol	0.79	Copper	8.9
Isopropanol	0.79	Gold	19.3
Methanol	0.79	Iron	7.9
Water	1.00	Lead	11.3
Gases (at 20°C and atmospheric pressure)		Lithium	0.53
Carbon dioxide	0.0018	Mercury	13.6
Oxygen	0.0013	Nickel	8.9
Nitrogen	0.0012	Silver	10.5
Helium	0.00017	Water (ice)	0.92
Hydrogen	0.000084	Zinc	7.1

Procedure:

1. Pour a few drops of cooking oil into a glass of water. Does the cooking oil sink or float in water? Do you think the density of cooking oil is more or less than 1.0 g/mL?

2. Carry out an experiment to test your prediction about the density of cooking oil. What do you find? Was your prediction correct?

3. Would density be useful in distinguishing among the alcohols known as methanol, ethanol, and isopropanol?

Densities of Sodas

Is it possible to determine the relative densities of various sodas?

Procedure:

1. Obtain four aluminum cans of cola. You will need regular cola (which contains caffeine and sugar), decaffeinated cola (with sugar), decaffeinated diet cola (no sugar or caffeine), and diet cola with caffeine.

2. Place the can of regular cola in a pail of water. Does it sink or float?

   What does this tell you about the density of a can of regular cola as compared with the density of water?

3. Next, place a can of decaffeinated diet cola in the water. Does it sink or float?

Results and Conclusions

Any difference in density could be due to the caffeine, the sugar, or both. Carry out an experiment to determine whether the difference in the density of sodas is caused by caffeine, sugar, or both. What do you find?

Based on the way they float or sink, you can estimate the densities of the different kinds of soda in grams per milliliter. Design experiments to test your estimates.

Did your estimates agree closely with the densities you measured? Which of the solids listed in Table 1 will float in water?

 Science Project Ideas

- Carry out an experiment to demonstrate that the volume of alcohol and water shrinks when these substances are mixed. Then try to develop a hypothesis to account for the shrinkage.

- Prepare sugar solutions of different concentrations by dissolving different weights of sugar in a fixed volume of water. How is the density of the sugar water related to the concentration of the solution? Is this also true of salt solutions?

EXPERIMENT 1.4

Using Density to Identify Solids

Question:

How can density be used to identify those solids whose irregular shapes make it difficult to calculate their volumes?

Hypothesis:

The volume of irregular objects can be determined by estimating how much water they displace.

Materials:

- ruler
- wood block
- balance
- water
- steel objects, such as washers, nuts, or bolts
- 100-mL graduated cylinder or metric measuring cup
- brass object
- cubes or cylinders of known metals, such as aluminum, copper, iron, lead, and zinc (optional)

To determine the density of a solid object, it's necessary to know its weight and volume. Often, the volume of a solid object can be easily obtained by measuring its dimensions. For example, you can use a ruler to measure the length, width, and height of a wooden block. As you probably know, the volume of such a block is equal to its length times its width times its height.

Procedure:

1. Find a block of wood and determine its volume (volume = length × width × height).

2. Weigh the block of wood. Now you can calculate its density. Remember that density = weight ÷ volume.

3. Compare the density of the wood with the density of water. Do you think the wood will sink or float in water?

4. Place it in water. Were you right?

The volumes of other solids, such as stones, cannot be measured easily. Their volumes can be found, however, by displacing water.

You can also use displacement to find the density of some steel objects, such as washers, nuts, and bolts.

Procedure:

1. Gather a number of identical steel washers, nuts, or bolts and weigh them.

2. Carefully drop the objects into a 100-mL graduated cylinder that holds, 50 mL of water. If the water rises to the 85-mL line, you know the volume of the washers is 35 mL (85 mL — 50 mL). Once you've found the volume, you can calculate the density, which is weight divided by volume.

Results and Conclusions

Like many metal products, steel is an alloy, a combination of metals. Steels are primarily iron, but they contain small amounts of carbon (a nonmetal) and possibly other metals that include nickel, chromium, molybdenum, vanadium, and tungsten. By how much does the density of the steel you measured differ from the density of iron given in Table 1?

Brass is an alloy of copper and zinc. Find a brass object and determine its density. Then, from Table 1 and what you learned in the previous experiment, determine the approximate percentage of zinc and copper in the brass object.

If possible, obtain some cubes or cylinders of known metals, such as aluminum, copper, iron, lead, and zinc. (Your school's science department may have such samples that you might borrow.) Find the densities of these metals and compare your findings with the densities listed in Table 1. How closely do your results agree with those in the table?

💡 Science Project Ideas

- Do different kinds of wood, such as pine, oak, maple, and birch, have different densities? Design and carry out experiments to find out.

- Find some pieces of copper (pipe, nails, or tubing), aluminum (bars, nails, tubing, or flashing), lead and zinc (flashing), and other metals. Find the densities of these metals. Then figure out whether they are pure metals or alloys.

EXPERIMENT 1.5

The Density of Pennies, New and Old

Question:

Modern pennies are made to exactly the same dimensions—they have the same volume. But are some more dense than others?

Hypothesis:

The metals used in pennies changed in 1982, so there will be a difference in densities before and after that year.

Materials:

- pennies minted before and after 1982, at least 40 of each kind
- balance
- 100-mL graduated cylinder or metric measuring cup
- water

Procedure:

1. Gather as many pennies as you can. You need a lot of pennies so that you can measure their volume accurately. The volume of just a few pennies is so small that it is difficult to measure accurately.

2. Separate the pennies into those minted before 1982 and those minted after 1982. The date is on the right side of each coin's face. A hundred of each type would be good, but 40–50 of each kind will be enough.

3. Weigh and record the weight of the pennies minted before 1982. Do the same for the pennies minted after 1982.

4. Next, find the volume of the pennies minted before 1982 by adding them to about 60 mL of water in a graduated cylinder. What is the volume of these pennies? What is the density of these pennies?

5. In the same way, find the volume of the pennies minted after 1982. What is the density of these pennies? How does the density of pennies minted after 1982 compare with the density of the pennies minted before 1982?

Results and Conclusions

Pennies are made from an alloy of copper and zinc. What must have happened to the composition of the alloy after 1982? Which pennies do you think contain more copper? What makes you think so? (See Table 1.)

Science Project Ideas

- Do some research to find the composition of pennies minted before 1982 and the change in composition that was made in 1982. Based on those compositions, calculate the expected densities of the two types of pennies.

- Design and carry out an experiment to determine whether or not nickels (5-cent coins) are really made of nickel.

- Dimes, quarters, half-dollars, and silver dollars are often referred to as silver coins. Design and carry out some experiments to find out whether or not these coins really are made of silver.

EXPERIMENT 1.6

Identification by Melting

Question:

How can exposing a substance to heat help identify it?

Hypothesis:

Every substance has a different melting point, so some melt at a lower temperature than others.

Materials:

- **an adult**
- 2 pairs of safety goggles
- small pieces of ice, candle wax, aluminum foil, iron wire, copper wire, sulfur (small lumps), lead foil
- oven mitt
- tongs
- matches
- candle
- Bunsen burner (from a science class)
- old pan

Safety: *This experiment should be done under adult supervision because you'll be working with flames. Wear safety goggles!*

Procedure:

1. Obtain small pieces of as many of the following substances as possible: ice, candle wax, aluminum foil, iron wire, copper wire, sulfur (small lumps), and lead foil.

Figure 4.

Have **an adult** hold the Bunsen burner at an angle to prevent melted matter from falling into it.

2. Wearing an oven mitt and using tongs, hold each piece, in turn, near the top of a candle flame. Which substances melt? Which do not melt?

3. Repeat the experiment using a Bunsen burner flame. To prevent any melted material from falling into the burner, **have the adult** hold the burner at an angle as shown in Figure 4. Place an old pan beneath the flame to catch any melted matter that may fall.

Results and Conclusions

Which substances melt? Which do not melt? Which of the substances melt at temperatures equal to or below the temperature of the candle flame? Which of the substances melt at a temperature between that of the candle and Bunsen burner flames? Which might melt at temperatures higher than the Bunsen burner flame (about 1,800°C)?

EXPERIMENT 1.7

The Melting and Freezing Temperature of Water (Ice)

Question:

Do substances melt at the same temperature at which they freeze?

Hypothesis:

Yes, and the same is true of boiling and condensation temperatures.

Materials:

- 12-oz Styrofoam cup
- chopped ice or snow
- thermometer that can measure temperatures at and below 0°C (32°F)
- plastic pail
- graduated cylinder or metric measuring cup
- freezer
- water
- 7-oz Styrofoam cup
- tape or clay
- notebook and pen or pencil
- clock or watch
- graph paper

Many substances melt and freeze at a particular temperature, known as the melting or freezing point. It's not necessary to list melting and freezing points separately because a substance freezes at the same temperature that it melts. The only difference is that to make a substance melt, heat is added; to make it freeze, heat is removed.

This also holds true for temperatures at which a substance boils or condenses. Many substances change on their own from liquid to gas (boil) at a particular temperature if heat is being added. If heat is being removed, the gas condenses to a liquid at a temperature known as its condensation point. For any particular substance, its boiling and condensation points are the same temperature.

As Table 2 reveals, melting (or freezing) temperatures can often be used to help identify substances. In this experiment, you'll measure the temperature at which solid water (ice) melts. You'll then check to see that it freezes at the same temperature that it melts.

Procedure:

1. Half fill a 12-oz Styrofoam cup with chopped ice or snow.

2. With a thermometer that can measure temperatures at and below 0°C (32°F), gently stir the ice or snow. What is the lowest temperature the ice or snow reaches as you stir it?

3. Continue to stir the cold solid for several minutes. Does the temperature change or does it remain about the same? According to your thermometer, at what temperature does solid water (ice or snow) melt? Bear in mind that common thermometers are only accurate to within one or two degrees of the true temperature.

4. Next, half fill a plastic pail with chopped ice or some snow, and then stir the solid particles with a thermometer. Does the amount of melting solid affect the temperature at which it changes to liquid?

Table 2.

The Melting (or Freezing) and Boiling (or Condensation) Temperatures of Some Common Substances

Substance	Melting (freezing) temperature (°C)	Boiling (condensation) temperature (°C)
Acetone	–95	57
Aluminum	658	1,800
Copper	1,084	2,310
Ethanol	–117	78.5
Helium	–272 (under pressure)	–269
Hydrogen	–259	–253
Iron	1,535	2,450
Isopropanol	–89	82
Lead	327	1,740
Methanol	–98	64.7
Nitrogen	–210	–196
Oxygen	–218	–183
Sodium	371	1,156
Sulfur	386	718

5. To see that water freezes at the same temperature at which it melts, first measure the temperature of the freezer you will use to freeze the water. It may take a few minutes for the thermometer to cool to the temperature of the freezer.

6. Pour about 50 mL of water into a 7-oz Styrofoam cup.

7. Place a thermometer in the water. Use tape or clay, as shown in Figure 5, to ensure that the thermometer bulb is slightly below the center of the volume of water.

8. Record the temperature of the water in your notebook.

9. Put the cup with the water and thermometer in a freezer where you can read the thermometer every 10 minutes by simply opening the freezer door.

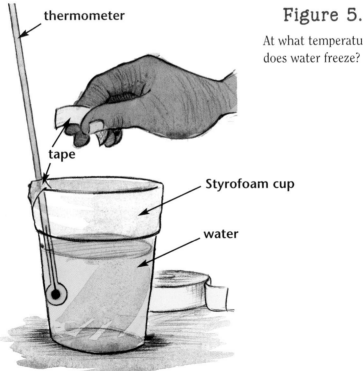

thermometer

tape

Figure 5.

At what temperature does water freeze?

Styrofoam cup

water

Continue to record the temperature of the water (and ice) until the temperature reaches the temperature of the freezer. What happens to the temperature while the water is freezing? What happens to the temperature after the water is frozen? Why does the temperature finally reach a minimum (lowest point)?

10. Leave the frozen water and thermometer in the freezer overnight. The next day, remove the frozen water from the freezer. Record its temperature at 10-minute intervals until it reaches room temperature.

11. Using the data you've collected, plot graphs of temperature and time for the water as it cooled and froze and for the ice as it melted and warmed. You can plot both graphs on the same set of axes. Place *time* on the x-axis and *temperature* on the y-axis.

Results and Conclusions

How does the graph of the water that froze compare with the graph of the ice that melted?

The author did a similar experiment with moth flakes (naphthalene). **Safety:** *Moth flakes are noxious without being heated.* He placed the flakes in a test tube, which he placed in a beaker of warm water until they melted. He then suspended a thermometer in the liquid. He recorded the temperature at one-minute intervals and used the data he collected to plot the graph shown in Figure 6.

What is the freezing temperature of naphthalene? What was the temperature of the room in which the experiment took place? If the author had heated the water to remelt the solid, what would that graph have looked like?

Examine Table 2. Which of the substances listed in the table are liquids at room temperature (20°C)? Which are solids? Which are gases?

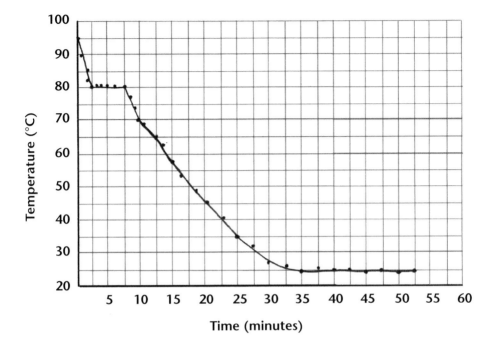

Figure 6.

A temperature and time graph for the freezing of moth flakes (naphthalene).

 Science Project Ideas

- **Under adult supervision,** carry out an experiment to find the freezing temperature of acetamide (C_2H_5NO).

- Some plumbers claim that pipes containing hot water will freeze before pipes that hold cold water. Can you find any evidence to support this claim?

- Why do the machines used to clean and make new ice in hockey rinks spray *hot* water on the ice?

EXPERIMENT 1.8

The Boiling Temperature of Water

Question:

How can you find the boiling temperature of water?

Hypothesis:

Using a thermometer to monitor the change in temperature, you can heat water until it reaches its boiling point.

Materials:

- **an adult**
- 2 pairs of safety goggles
- small cooking pan
- cold water
- hot plate or stove
- thermometer with range of –10°C to 110°C
- notebook and pen or pencil
- clock or watch
- graph paper

Safety: *Do this experiment under adult supervision. You should both wear safety goggles.*

Procedure:

1. Half fill a small cooking pan with cold water.

2. Put a thermometer that has a scale extending from −10°C to 110°C in the water (see Figure 7). What is the temperature of the cold water? Record the temperature in your notebook.

3. Turn on a hot plate or one of the small heating elements on a stove.

Figure 7.

You can heat water on a hot plate or stove to find its boiling temperature.

4. Next, put the pan of water with the thermometer in it on the hot plate or heating element.

5. As the water warms, record the water temperature at one-minute intervals.

   Also, note the small bubbles that form and rise to the surface. Some are bubbles of air that were dissolved in the water. You have probably seen such air bubbles in a cold glass of water that was left overnight. But other bubbles form when liquid water changes to gas. When the water begins to boil, the bubbles of gaseous water rise to the surface and burst. What is the temperature of the water when it begins to boil vigorously? (Be careful not to let the thermometer bulb touch the pan.)

6. Continue heating the water and recording its temperature until about half of it has boiled away into a gas.

7. According to your measurements, what is the boiling temperature of water? Plot a temperature and time graph of your data. How can you account for the shape of the graph?

Results and Conclusions

The author heated a small volume of an alcohol to boiling using the equipment shown in Figure 8a. The apparatus enabled him to find the boiling temperature without allowing the gaseous alcohol to reach the flame. This was important because alcohol is flammable.

He boiled away most of the alcohol and condensed it in a test tube immersed in cold water. While doing the experiment, he recorded the temperature of the heated alcohol over a period of time. He then plotted a graph of the data, which is shown in Figure 8b. From his graph and Table 2, which alcohol do you think he heated? Why do you think so?

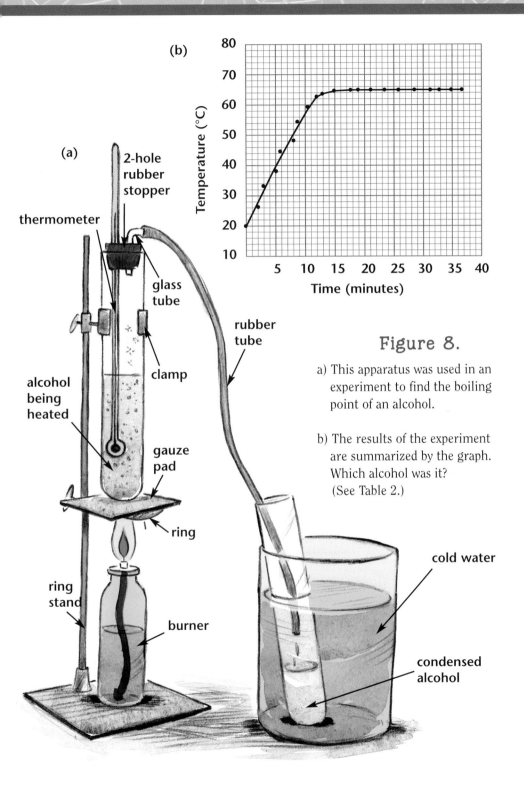

(a)

thermometer

2-hole
rubber
stopper

glass
tube

clamp

alcohol
being
heated

gauze
pad

ring

rubber
tube

ring
stand

burner

cold water

condensed
alcohol

(b)

Temperature (°C)

Time (minutes)

Figure 8.

a) This apparatus was used in an
   experiment to find the boiling
   point of an alcohol.

b) The results of the experiment
   are summarized by the graph.
   Which alcohol was it?
   (See Table 2.)

Science Project Ideas

- People living in Denver, Colorado, say that water there boils at about 95°C. Can this be true? If it is true, how can it be explained?

- Do some research to find out why the boiling point of water is so much higher than other compounds of comparable atomic weight, such as ammonia, methane, and hydrogen sulfide.

EXPERIMENT 1.9

Using Solubility to Identify Substances

Question:

How can solubility identify a substance?

Hypothesis:

Substances often widely differ in how they dissolve (disappear) when mixed in another substance. This characteristic identifies them from one another.

Materials:

- teaspoon
- sugar
- drinking glasses
- graduated cylinder or metric measuring cup
- water
- ¼ teaspoon kosher salt
- methanol (methyl alcohol)
- Epsom salt (magnesium sulfate)
- citric acid
- baking soda, baking powder, flour, instant tea, instant coffee, Kool-Aid drink powder, Tang drink powder, vitamin C, aspirin, gelatin, and cornstarch

Solubility is a property that is used to identify substances. If one substance dissolves when mixed in another, we say it is soluble in that substance. If little or none of the solid dissolves, we say it is insoluble.

Procedure:

1. Add one teaspoon of sugar to a drinking glass.

2. Add about 100 mL of warm water and stir the mixture. Does sugar dissolve in water?

3. Repeat the experiment with kosher salt. Does salt dissolve in water?

4. Try dissolving ¼ teaspoon of each of the following, one at a time, in half a glass of water: baking soda, baking powder, flour, instant tea, instant coffee, Kool-Aid drink powder, Tang drink powder, vitamin C, aspirin, gelatin, and cornstarch.

Results and Conclusions

Which substances are soluble in water? Which are insoluble? Are any of the insoluble substances soluble in hot water?

Sugar and citric acid are both white powders with about the same densities. You know that sugar is soluble in water. Is citric acid also soluble? To find out, add a pinch of citric acid to some water and stir. What do you conclude?

Is either of these solids soluble in methanol (methyl alcohol)? To find out, add a pinch of each to separate glasses that contain some methanol and stir. Did either dissolve?

What about Epsom salt (magnesium sulfate)? Is it soluble in water? In methanol?

Science Project Ideas

- Design and carry out experiments to find the maximum weight of kosher salt, Epsom salt, and sugar that can be dissolved in 100 mL of water at room temperature. Which solid is most soluble? Which is least soluble?

- Carry out additional experiments to determine how temperature affects the solubility of these solids in water. Then plot graphs of solubility, in grams per 100 mL of water, vs. temperature.

- Find the weight of salt that is dissolved in 100 mL of seawater.

- Design and carry out experiments to find the freezing temperatures of saturated solutions of salt, Epsom salt, and sugar.

- Do you think a bouillon cube will dissolve faster in hot water or cold water? Design and carry out an experiment to find out.

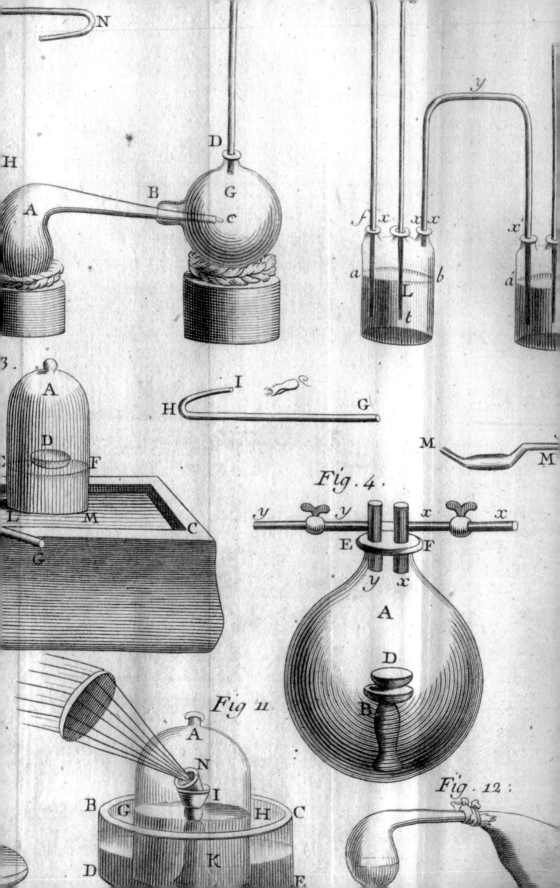

Fig. 4.

Fig. 11

Fig. 12

CHAPTER 2

Conservation of Matter

The scientific law of the conservation of matter states that there is no gain or loss of weight during physical or chemical changes. Antoine Lavoisier, a French scientist, was to eighteenth-century chemistry what Isaac Newton had been to seventeenth-century physics. It was Lavoisier who combined the major useful ideas of chemistry, demonstrated the false assumptions of other concepts, provided new and unifying ideas of his own, and made careful weighings and measurements the basis of chemistry. It was Lavoisier, too, who developed a practical language and system for naming elements and compounds.

Lavoisier weighed a large number of chemicals before and after physical and chemical changes. In all the experiments he did, he could find no change in weight. In the next two experiments, see if your results confirm what Lavoisier found.

◄ This 1789 illustration shows scientific instruments used to prepare hydrogen. It was drawn by Marie Anne Paulze, the wife of chemist Antoine Lavoisier.

EXPERIMENT 2.1

Does Heat Have Weight?

Question:

When water freezes and loses heat does its weight change?

Hypothesis:

There will be no change. You can find out by first weighing water as liquid, then weighing the same water as ice.

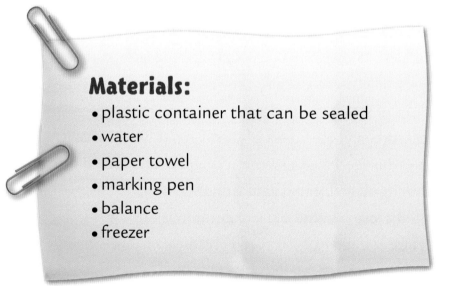

Materials:

- plastic container that can be sealed
- water
- paper towel
- marking pen
- balance
- freezer

We can understand that water loses heat when it freezes. But does heat have weight? If it does, we might expect that ice would weigh less than the water that froze.

Procedure:

1. To test this idea, find a plastic container that you can seal. Partially fill the container with water and seal it. Be sure to wipe off any moisture that may be on the outside of the container.

2. With a marking pen, draw a short line at the water level in the container. Then weigh the container as accurately as you can.

3. Next, place the container in a freezer and allow the water to freeze overnight.

4. The next day you can remove the container from the freezer. Wipe off any moisture that may condense on the cold container.

5. Quickly weigh the container.

Results and Conclusions

Has the container lost weight? Notice the level of the ice in the container. What happened to the volume when the water froze?

Do you think the weight will change after the ice melts back to water?

After the ice melts, wipe off any moisture that may have condensed on the outside of the container and weigh it again. What do you find? Do your results match Lavoisier's?

Science Project Idea

- Design and carry out an experiment to see if there is any change in weight when salt or sugar dissolves in water.

EXPERIMENT 2.2

Lavoisier and a Chemical Law

Question:

Does a chemical change alter the weight of the substances involved in the process?

Hypothesis:

Even though a new substance is formed by chemical change, nothing is added or removed, so the weight will remain the same.

Materials:

- **an adult**
- paper
- balance
- graduated cylinder
- distilled water
- small containers or beakers
- straws
- marking pen and tape
- plastic vials and caps
- lead nitrate [$Pb(NO_3)_2$] and sodium iodide (**ask an adult**, perhaps a science teacher, to obtain these chemicals for you)

Safety: *In this experiment you will use chemicals that are poisonous if ingested. Consequently, you should work with a knowledgeable adult.*

In Experiment 2.1, you probably found there was no change in weight when water changed from liquid to solid as it froze. That was a physical change because no new substances were formed.

Lavoisier weighed a large number of chemicals before and after chemical and physical changes. In all the experiments he did, he could find no change in weight. In this experiment, you will measure the weight before and after a chemical change, one in which new substances are formed.

Procedure:

1. Place a small piece of paper on a balance pan.

2. Weigh out 7.5 g of lead nitrate.

3. On a separate piece of paper, weigh out 3.5 g of sodium iodide.

4. Prepare a clear solution by adding the lead nitrate and 50 mL of distilled water to a small container or beaker and stirring with a straw.

5. Prepare a second clear solution in another small container by adding sodium iodide to 50 mL of distilled water. Label the solutions.

6. Fill a plastic vial about one third of the way with one of the solutions. Pour about the same amount of the other solution into a different vial. Place caps on both vials to avoid evaporation or spilling.

7. Weigh the two vials and their contents together on a balance.

8. Carefully remove the covers from the vials and pour one solution into the other. Be careful not to lose any liquid.

9. Replace the caps on both vials, place them on the balance, and reweigh them.

Results and Conclusions

What evidence is there that a chemical change has taken place? Has the chemical change been accompanied by a change in weight?

 Science Project Idea

- Design and carry out, **under adult supervision,** an experiment to show that even when a gas forms in a chemical reaction, the law of the conservation of matter holds true.

Dalton and the Atomic Theory

Although Lavoisier made important discoveries in chemistry, he never developed a theory to explain the laws of nature that he and others discovered. It was John Dalton who first crafted a theory to explain the laws of chemistry.

Dalton was an English chemist who worked in the early 1800s. Like other chemists of that time, he knew that elements were pure substances and that different elements could combine to form compounds. To explain what made an element pure, Dalton developed what has come to be known as the atomic theory. He proposed that all matter is made up of tiny, indivisible, indestructible particles called atoms. According to his theory, the atoms of any one element are identical to each other but different from the atoms of any other element. Atoms of different elements differ in weight. And since atoms are indestructible, there is no change in weight when substances undergo physical or chemical change.

To find the relative weights of atoms, he "decomposed" compounds—reducing them into their separate elements and weighing them. Or he weighed the elements that combined to form the compound. For example, by passing an electric current through water, he was able to separate water into the gases hydrogen and oxygen. This resulted in the release of eight grams of oxygen for every one gram of hydrogen. If one gram of hydrogen was mixed with eight grams of oxygen and

John Dalton
(1766–1844)

ignited with a spark, an explosion took place. After the explosion, nine grams of water and no gas remained.

Based on this evidence, Dalton concluded that oxygen atoms weigh eight times as much as hydrogen atoms. He assumed that hydrogen and oxygen combine to form water in a 1:1 ratio. Therefore, he concluded, the molecular formula for water was HO.

Avogardo's Hypothesis

Later, an Italian chemist, Amedio Avogadro, hypothesized that equal volumes of gases at the same temperature and pressure contain the same number of molecules. Since for any given volume of oxygen, twice that volume of hydrogen combines with it, Avogadro concluded that the formula for water was H_2O. Today we know that Avogadro was right. However, it took half a century before his hypothesis and conclusion about the formula for water was accepted by most chemists.

Now, since hydrogen gas is the lightest (least dense) gas known, chemists assigned hydrogen atoms a relative weight of one unit (1 atomic mass unit, or 1 amu). No one knew what the actual weight of an atom was because atoms were too light to be weighed. However, if hydrogen atoms weighed 1 amu, oxygen atoms must weigh 16 amu. After all, two grams of hydrogen combine with 16 grams of oxygen, a ratio of 1:8. Since two atoms of hydrogen combine with one atom of oxygen, a ratio of 2:1, the oxygen atoms must be 16 times as heavy as the hydrogen atoms in order for their weight ratio in water to be 1:8.

$$2 \times \frac{1}{16} = \frac{2}{16} = \frac{1}{8}$$

Today we know not only the relative weights of the atoms of every element, we know their actual weights as well. The relative and actual weights of some common elements are shown in Table 3.

Table 3.
The Relative and Actual Weights of the Atoms of Some Common Elements*

Element	Relative weight of atom in atomic mass units (amu)	Actual weight in septillionths of a gram**
Hydrogen	1.0	1.7
Helium	4.0	6.7
Carbon	12.0	20
Oxygen	16.0	27
Sodium	23.0	38.3
Magnesium	24.3	40.5
Aluminum	27.0	45
Sulfur	32.1	53.5
Chlorine	35.5	59
Iron	55.8	93
Copper	63.5	106
Zinc	65.4	109
Lead	207	345

* Based on oxygen atoms having an atomic weight of 16 amu.
** A septillionth of a gram is 0.0000000000000000000000001 gram.

EXPERIMENT 2.3

Paper Clips, Washers, "Chemical Formulas," and Laws of Nature

Question:

Can a model of a chemical compound show what happens when its molecules are "decomposed" into atoms?

Hypothesis:

By dividing the model's "atoms" into groups you can see how molecules decompose.

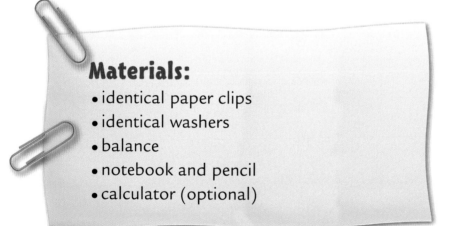

Materials:

- identical paper clips
- identical washers
- balance
- notebook and pencil
- calculator (optional)

The smallest particle of a compound is a molecule. It contains atoms of the elements that combine to form the compound. A chemical formula, such as H_2O, tells the ratio of the atoms of the elements that make up the compound. In a molecule of water, there are two atoms of hydrogen for every one atom of oxygen.

This experiment provides a concrete look at how chemists arrive at chemical formulas and two laws of nature. You will use identical paper clips to represent atoms of an imaginary element C and identical washers to represent atoms of element W.

Procedure:

1. Prepare a large number of "molecules" (at least 10) of CW by joining "atoms" of C (paper clips) and W (washers) as shown in Figure 9a.

2. Place all the molecules on a balance pan.

3. Record the weight of the "compound" you have prepared.

4. Next, "decompose" the compound into the elements C and W as shown in Figure 9b.

5. Place the atoms of both elements on the same balance pan you used before and record the weight.

Results and Conclusions

What is the total weight of the elements? Compare the total weight of the two elements with the weight of the compound you prepared.

How do your weighings illustrate the law of conservation of matter? That is, how do they illustrate that matter is neither created nor destroyed in a chemical reaction?

Now weigh separately each of the elements that you obtained by decomposing the compound. What is the weight of C? What is the

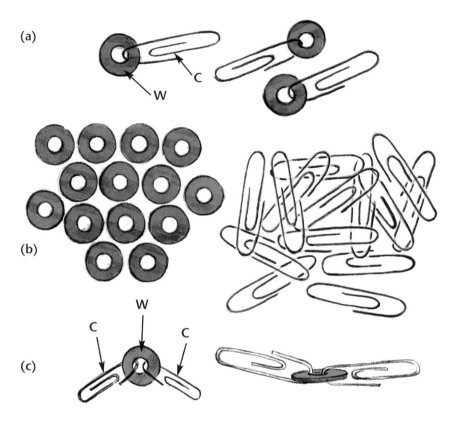

Figure 9.

a) Prepare some molecules of the "compound" CW.
   Then weigh the compound.
b) Decompose the compound into its elements, C and W.
c) Prepare molecules of the "compound" C_2W.

weight of W? What is the relative weight of an atom of W to an atom of C? For example, if you combined 12 grams of paper clips with 36 grams of washers, the relative weight of washers to paper clips would be:

$$W{:}C = 36{:}12 = 36 \div 12 : 12 \div 12 = 3{:}1$$

If the weight of an atom of C is considered to be 10 amu, what is the weight of an atom of W in amu?

What was the percentage composition of the compound CW? To find out, first divide the weight, in grams, of element C by the weight of the compound CW. Why should you multiply that decimal fraction by 100 to find the percentage? How can you find the percentage of W in the same compound?

Procedure:

1. Repeat the experiment, but prepare only about half as many molecules of the compound CW.

2. Again, record the weight of the "compound."

3. Decompose the compound into the elements C and W.

Results and Conclusions

What was the percentage composition of the compound? How do the results of these two experiments illustrate the law of constant proportions? That is, how do the results demonstrate that elements always combine to form a particular compound in a fixed percentage, or ratio, by weight?

Multiple Proportions

Suppose, as is often true in nature, that elements C and W combine to form more than one compound. Use the same "atoms" of C and W to prepare as many molecules as possible of the compound C_2W (2 Cs and 1 W), as shown in Figure 9c. The formula C_2W shows that there are two atoms of C and one atom of W in each molecule of C_2W. This formula is similar to the formula H_2O, which also shows there are two atoms of hydrogen and one atom of oxygen in each molecule of water. What is the percentage of C in the compound C_2W? What is the percentage of W?

Chemists have found that carbon and oxygen combine to form two different gases. In one (carbon monoxide), the ratio of carbon to oxygen is 3:4; in the other (carbon dioxide), the ratio is 3:8. For a fixed weight of carbon, let's say 3, the ratio of oxygen in carbon monoxide to oxygen in carbon dioxide is 4:8, or more simply, 1:2.

In all cases where two elements combine to form more than one compound, the following law of multiple proportions holds true: If the weight of one element is kept the same, the ratio of the weight of the other element in the two or more compounds will be in simple whole numbers. For carbon monoxide and carbon dioxide, when the weight of carbon is fixed, the ratio of oxygen in the two compounds is 1:2. For other compounds, it might be 3:2, 5:2, and so on, but the ratios are always simple whole numbers.

How does this experiment, in which you made the compounds CW and C_2W, illustrate the law of multiple proportions? Predict the percentage composition of the compound CW_2. Then carry out an experiment to confirm your prediction. Do the same for the compound C_2W_3. Were your predictions correct? If not, can you figure out where you made a mistake? How do the compounds CW, C_2W, CW_2, and C_2W_3 illustrate the law of multiple proportions?

Antoine Lavoisier, a Great Chemist

Many of the basic ideas and experiments that led to the law of conservation of mass were conceived of or performed by the great French scientist Antoine Lavoisier.

Lavoisier had the good fortune to marry Marie Anne Paulze, a woman who illustrated his books, translated books and letters, helped him with experiments, and recorded his notes. Marie Lavoisier was one of the few women we know was involved in science prior to the twentieth century.

Lavoisier lived during the time of the French Revolution—a time of great violent change in French society. To support his experimental work, Lavoisier worked as a tax collector. Many tax collectors were persecuted by the French revolutionary forces, and Lavoisier was among those arrested. When he pleaded that he was a scientist and not a tax collector,

Marie and Antoine Lavoisier

the radical, antimonarchist judge replied, "The Republic has no need of scientists." And so, on May 8, 1794, Lavoisier and his father-in-law (also a tax collector) were beheaded. Lavoisier's friend, astronomer Joseph-Louis Lagrange, spoke for the future when he said of Lavoisier: "It took but a moment to cut off his head; it will take a century to produce another like it."

CHAPTER 3

Some Chemical Reactions and Their Reaction Speeds

A chemical reaction in which oxygen combines with other substances to form compounds is called oxidation. You see oxidation every time something burns. Burning is rapid oxidation, but not all oxidation reactions are so speedy. The rusting of iron is an example of slow oxidation that you will examine in Experiment 3.1.

◄A car abandoned in the ghost town of Bodie, California, is covered with rust. Rust is the result of the chemical reaction called oxidation.

EXPERIMENT 3.1

Rusting of Iron

Question:

Does iron always oxidize (rust) at the same rate when exposed to oxygen and liquids?

Hypothesis:

Iron oxidizes at different rates depending on the chemicals with which it comes in contact.

Materials:

- **safety goggles**
- steel wool (without soap)
- scissors
- water
- household ammonia
- vinegar
- cups or glasses
- spoon
- paper towels
- marking pen
- soap and water

Iron (Fe) rusts when oxygen in the air slowly combines with it to form a compound called iron, or ferric, oxide (Fe_2O_3). You can use steel wool, which contains iron, to study this process.

Procedure:

1. To see how different chemicals may affect the rate of rusting, **put on safety goggles**, then cut a steel wool pad (one without soap) into four equal parts.

2. Soak one piece in water, one in ammonia, and a third in vinegar. The fourth piece can remain dry. It can serve as a control.

3. After soaking the pieces of steel wool for several minutes, remove them using a spoon and put them on labeled paper towels. **Then wash your hands thoroughly.**

4. Leave the samples for at least a day. Then examine them periodically to see what happens.

Results and Conclusions

Which piece is the first to show evidence of rusting? Do any appear not to rust at all? Record your results and save them for analysis in Chapter 5, Experiment 5.5.

EXPERIMENT 3.2

The Percentage of Oxygen in Air

Question:

How can you determine the percentage of oxygen in air?

Hypothesis:

By using iron to remove oxygen from air, you can measure the percentage of oxygen in air.

Materials:

- steel wool pad (without soap)
- drinking glasses
- vinegar
- water
- shallow plastic container
- ruler
- food coloring
- 2 narrow jars (olive jars are good) or large test tubes
- rubber bands
- pencil
- paper
- marking pen

Procedure:

1. Begin by soaking a pad of steel wool in a glass of vinegar for 20 minutes. While the steel wool is soaking, add water to a depth of about 2 centimeters to a shallow plastic container. To make the water more visible, you can add a few drops of food coloring.

2. Pull a few strands of steel wool from the pad that has soaked in vinegar. Roll them into a small, loosely packed ball. The ball should be slightly wider than the diameter of the narrow jar (an olive jar is good) or large test tube you plan to use.

3. Put the steel wool ball into one of the narrow jars or test tubes. Use a pencil to push the ball all the way to the bottom of the jar or tube.

4. Push a ball of paper to the bottom of the second tube or jar.

5. Turn the tubes upside down and place them side by side in the container of water you prepared earlier, as shown in Figure 10. Devise some means of fastening the tubes so they won't tip over.

6. Leave the inverted tubes for a period of 24 hours. As the oxygen in the air reacts with the steel wool, water should rise up the tube, replacing the volume previously occupied by the gas.

7. After 24 hours, mark the water level in each tube with a marking pen or a rubber band. Leave them for several more hours to see if the water level rises any higher.

Figure 10.

What fraction of air is oxygen?

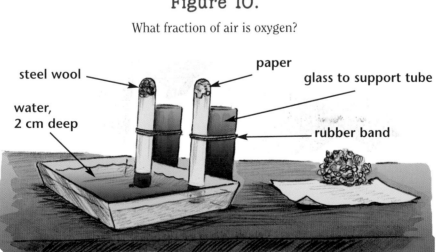

8. Once the water level has stopped rising, look closely at the steel wool in the tube. Has it rusted? Did the water rise in the tube that held the ball of paper? What was the purpose of that tube?

9. Use the ruler to measure the height of the water in the tube that contains the steel wool. What is the ratio of the height of the water level to the total height of the tube?

Results and Conclusions

According to your measurements, what fraction of the air is oxygen? What percentage of air is oxygen? For example, suppose water rises to a height of 3 cm in a jar that is 15 cm tall. The fraction and percentage of the air that is oxygen would be:

$$\frac{3 \text{ cm}}{15 \text{ cm}} = \frac{1}{5} = 0.2 = 20\%$$

 Science Project Ideas

- Design and carry out an experiment to see whether placing the steel wool at different places in the jar or tube affects the height to which the water rises.

- Will a candle burning in a limited supply of air use up all the oxygen in the air before it goes out? Design an experiment to find out. Then, **under adult supervision,** carry out your experiment.

EXPERIMENT 3.3

Preparing and Testing Oxygen

Question:
How can you test the properties of oxygen?

Hypothesis:
Oxygen can be prepared using hydrogen peroxide, and tested using a few different methods.

Materials:
- **an adult**
- 2 pairs of safety goggles
- half-pint bottles
- one-hole rubber stopper that fits the mouth of a bottle
- short length of glass tubing
- soap or glycerin
- rubber tubing
- plastic pail
- water
- square pieces of cardboard or rigid plastic
- 100-mL graduated cylinder
- teaspoon
- 3% hydrogen peroxide solution (from a pharmacy or supermarket)
- manganese dioxide (from science teacher or science supply company)
- wood splint
- matches
- tongs
- steel wool (without soap)
- Bunsen burner (use in school science room)
- sink

The decomposition of hydrogen peroxide (H_2O_2) is normally very slow, but manganese dioxide will speed up the reaction. Manganese dioxide will serve as a catalyst. A catalyst is a substance that changes the rate of a reaction without itself undergoing any change. Oxygen, which you've probably found makes up about one fifth (20 percent) of air, can be tested for characteristics such as color, odor, and solubility in water.

Procedure:

1. To begin, obtain a half-pint bottle and a one-hole rubber stopper that fits the mouth of the bottle.

2. **Ask an adult** to insert a short length of glass tubing into the stopper. (A little soap or glycerin on the glass may make it easier to insert the tubing.)

3. Attach a piece of rubber tubing about 30 cm (1 ft) long to the glass tubing.

4. Next, fill a plastic pail about one third full with water. Fill another half-pint bottle with water and cover its mouth with a square piece of cardboard or rigid plastic.

5. Invert the bottle and put it in the pail. You can then remove the cover. Water will remain in the bottle as long as its mouth is beneath the surface of the water in the pail.

6. Remove the stopper from the upright bottle and pour 100 mL of a 3% hydrogen peroxide solution into the bottle.

7. Add one teaspoon of manganese dioxide to the hydrogen peroxide and replace the stopper.

8. Place the end of the rubber tubing into the pail. When gas bubbles begin to emerge from the tube, let them escape. They are mostly air that was in the flask and the tube. The air is being replaced by oxygen.

9. After about 30 seconds, place the end of the tube under the inverted water-filled bottle as shown in Figure 11.

10. While gas collects in the bottle, prepare a second bottle in which you can collect gas.

11. When the first bottle is filled with gas, slide the cardboard or plastic cover under it and remove it from the pail. Stand that covered bottle upright and place the tube under the second bottle in the pail. Collect a second bottle of oxygen. Cover it, remove it from the pail, and place it beside the first bottle.

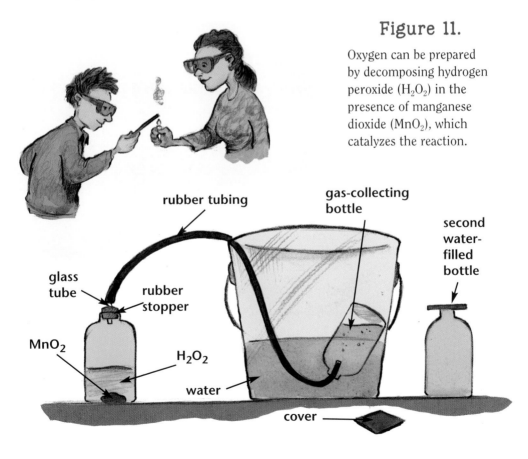

Figure 11.

Oxygen can be prepared by decomposing hydrogen peroxide (H_2O_2) in the presence of manganese dioxide (MnO_2), which catalyzes the reaction.

rubber tubing

gas-collecting bottle

second water-filled bottle

glass tube

rubber stopper

MnO_2

H_2O_2

water

cover

12. Put on safety goggles and, **under adult supervision**, light a wood splint. When it is burning well, blow it out.

13. Remove the cover from the bottle of oxygen and insert the glowing splint into the bottle of oxygen. What happens? Dip the splint into the pail of water to put it out.

14. Using tongs, hold a small ball of steel wool (without soap) in a Bunsen burner flame. When the steel is glowing, quickly place it in the second bottle of oxygen. What happens?

15. Place the steel wool in a sink where it can cool.

Predict what will happen if you remove the stopper from the bottle of H_2O_2 and insert a glowing splint into the bottle. **Under adult supervision**, try it! Was your prediction correct?

Results and Conclusions

Based on what you observed in this experiment, what can you say about oxygen's color, odor, and solubility in water? How does oxygen affect the rate at which something burns? How might you test a gas to see if it is oxygen?

 Science Project Ideas

- Cut a slice of potato into small pieces and put them in a flask. Then add about 50 mL of 3% hydrogen peroxide and swirl the flask. Is there evidence of a chemical reaction? Might the gas bubbles be oxygen? **Under adult supervision,** carry out a test to see if the gas is oxygen. What do you find?

- In addition to manganese dioxide, what other substances might serve as catalysts in the decomposition of hydrogen peroxide? You might begin with small pieces of raw beef liver.

- Why is hydrogen peroxide always stored in dark brown plastic bottles?

EXPERIMENT 3.4

The Rate at Which Hydrogen Peroxide Decomposes

Question:

What factors affect the rate of decomposition for hydrogen peroxide?

Hypothesis:

The rate at which hydrogen peroxide decomposes depends on how concentrated it is (in solution) and on the use of a catalyst.

Materials:

- **an adult**
- 2 pairs of safety goggles
- paper clips
- washers
- 3% hydrogen peroxide solution
- 100- or 150-mL flask
- clear plastic containers
- water
- 1-hole rubber stopper that fits flask
- short glass tube
- soap or glycerin
- rubber tubing
- 10- and 100-mL graduated cylinders
- square pieces of cardboard or rigid plastic
- clamp
- ring stand
- potassium iodide (KI) from science teacher or science supply company
- balance
- notebook and pencil
- clock or watch

The chemical formula for hydrogen peroxide is H_2O_2. This compound decomposes slowly to form water (H_2O) and oxygen (O_2). The reaction can be represented by the chemical equation

$$2H_2O_2 \longrightarrow 2H_2O + O_2$$

(Hydrogen peroxide yields water and oxygen.)

The formulas show that there are two atoms of hydrogen and two atoms of oxygen in each molecule of H_2O_2. The formulas also show that there are two atoms of hydrogen and one atom of oxygen in each molecule of water and two atoms of oxygen in each molecule of oxygen. In the equation, you see a 2 in front of the H_2O_2 and another 2 in front of the H_2O. These numbers are used to balance the equation. The word equation indicates an equality of numbers before and after the arrow. If you count the number of atoms of hydrogen and oxygen on either side of the arrow, you will find that four hydrogen atoms and four oxygen atoms are found on both sides of the arrow. To be realistic, equations have to be balanced because we know matter cannot be created or destroyed.

If the equation were written

$$H_2O_2 \longrightarrow H_2O + O_2$$

it would indicate that one molecule of oxygen and one molecule of water are created for every molecule of hydrogen peroxide that decomposes. Notice, however, that there are three atoms of oxygen on the right side of the equation and only two on the left side. This equation is not balanced: something is missing.

Procedure:

1. Using paper clips and washers to represent atoms of hydrogen and oxygen, prepare "molecules" that represent hydrogen peroxide.

2. Decompose these molecules into water and oxygen molecules. You will quickly see that two molecules of hydrogen peroxide are needed to form two molecules of water and one molecule of oxygen.

3. To observe the actual reaction, **put on your safety goggles** and pour 15 mL of a 3% hydrogen peroxide solution into a flask.

4. Place the flask in a clear plastic container that contains water at room temperature. The water will keep the reaction at a constant temperature.

   In this experiment you will test the effect of concentration (amount of hydrogen peroxide per volume) on the rate of the reaction. Temperature might also affect the speed of the reaction, so you need to keep the temperature constant. Otherwise, you wouldn't know if it was concentration or temperature that was affecting the rate.

5. **Ask an adult** to insert a short glass tube into a one-hole rubber stopper. (A little soap or glycerin on the glass may make insertion easier.)

6. Place the stopper in the flask and connect a piece of rubber tubing to the glass tube.

7. Place the end of the rubber tubing under an inverted 100-mL graduated cylinder that is filled with water. The open end of the cylinder should be under water in another plastic container to make sure that the water stays in the cylinder. If necessary, a clamp attached to a ring stand can be used to support the cylinder as shown in Figure 12.

Figure 12.

How fast does hydrogen peroxide (H_2O_2) decompose when potassium iodide (KI) is used as a catalyst?

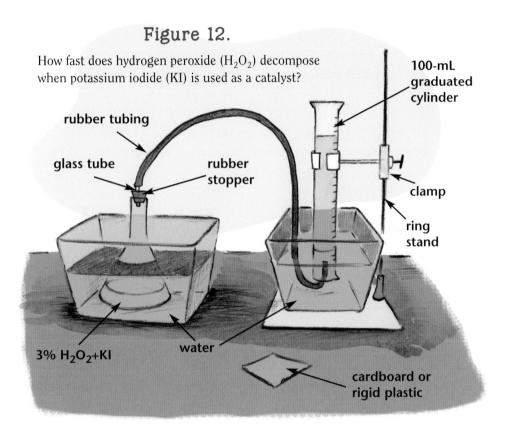

100-mL graduated cylinder

rubber tubing

glass tube

rubber stopper

clamp

ring stand

3% H_2O_2+KI

water

cardboard or rigid plastic

8. Swirl the flask and look for bubbles of oxygen to be released and collected in the graduated cylinder. As you can see, this reaction is a very slow one. In fact, you may not see any bubbles of gas.

Perhaps a catalyst will increase the rate of the reaction. A catalyst, as you have seen, is a substance that changes the rate of a reaction without undergoing any change itself.

9. To find out, prepare a catalyst by adding 3.3 grams of potassium iodide (KI) to 100 mL of water. After the solid has dissolved, remove the rubber tubing from beneath the graduated cylinder and the stopper from the flask.

10. **Ask an adult**, who is wearing safety goggles, to add 15 mL of the KI solution to the hydrogen peroxide in the flask. Replace the stopper and rubber tube as before and again swirl the flask. Continue to swirl the flask in the water bath throughout the experiment.

11. When bubbles of oxygen begin to collect, record the time. Record the time again when 10 mL of gas have formed. Continue to record the time after each additional 10 mL of gas have been collected. Do this until you have collected 80 to 100 mL of gas.

Results and Conclusions

What happens to the rate of the reaction as more gas is collected? What must happen to the concentration of hydrogen peroxide as the reaction proceeds? Based on your data, what can you conclude about the effect of the concentration of hydrogen peroxide on the rate of its decomposition? **Under adult supervision**, carry out a test to show that the gas you collected is oxygen.

 Science Project Idea

- Design and carry out an experiment to see if the concentration of the catalyst affects the rate at which hydrogen peroxide decomposes to water and oxygen.

EXPERIMENT 3.5

Influencing the Rate of a Reaction

Question:

Do external factors affect the speed of a chemical reaction?

Hypothesis:

Yes. Factors that affect chemical reactions include changes in temperature, the surface area being tested, and the concentration of the reactants.

Materials:

- hot and cold water
- clear plastic cups
- seltzer tablets
- paper
- watch or clock with a second hand

Rate vs. Temperature

As you saw in the previous experiment, the rate of a reaction depends on the concentration of the substances that react (the reactants). You may remember that you carried out the reaction in a water bath in order to keep the temperature constant. How do you think temperature might affect the speed of a chemical reaction?

Procedure:

1. Place equal amounts of hot and cold water in separate clear plastic cups.

2. Drop one seltzer tablet into each cup at the same time. You can use a watch or a clock with a second hand to compare the times for each tablet to completely disappear.

Results and Conclusions

In which cup does the reaction go faster? What effect does temperature have on the rate of this reaction?

Rate vs. Surface Area

Could the amount of surface area affect the rate of a reaction? To find out, you will need two seltzer tablets.

Procedure:

1. On a sheet of paper, crush one seltzer tablet into tiny pieces. How does this affect its surface area—the amount of surface exposed to other substances such as air or water? Leave the second tablet whole.

2. Drop both tablets at the same time into equal volumes of water at the same temperature in two separate but identical containers.

Results and Conclusions

Why should the water temperature be the same in both containers? Which tablet reacts faster? How does surface area affect the rate of a reaction?

Rate vs. Concentration of Reactants

In this reaction, seltzer and water are the reactants. The gas formed (carbon dioxide) and some soluble substances are the products. Do you think the speed of the reaction will depend on the amount (concentration) of seltzer used?

Procedure:

1. Drop a whole seltzer tablet into half a cup of water.

2. At the same time, drop half a tablet into an equal amount of water in an identical cup.

Results and Conclusions

In which container is gas produced faster? (Remember, if the reaction speed is the same in both containers, it will take the whole tablet exactly twice as long to react as the half tablet.) What do you find? Was your answer right?

Rate vs. Concentration of Products

If you drop a seltzer tablet into a cup of water where several tablets have already reacted, there will be a lot of the products of the reaction (the gas and new chemicals formed by the reaction) already in the water. Do you think this will affect the speed of the reaction between the seltzer and water?

Procedure:

1. You can increase the concentration of one of the products of the reaction, namely the gas, by placing the palm of your hand firmly over the top of the cup where the reaction is happening.

   This will prevent the gas from escaping and raise the concentration of gas and pressure above the liquid. How does this increase in concentration of a product affect the rate at which bubbles form? What happens to the rate of the reaction when you remove your hand?

2. To increase the concentration of the new substances and gas that remain in solution, drop a seltzer tablet into half a cup of water. When the tablet has completely disappeared, place a second half cup of water beside the first. Drop a seltzer tablet into each of the two cups.

Results and Conclusions

In which cup is the reaction speed greater? What can you conclude? Will the amount of water into which you put a seltzer tablet affect the speed of the reaction? Design an experiment to find out.

Science Project Ideas

- Examine the list of ingredients on a box of seltzer tablets. Obtain these ingredients. Then carry out experiments to find out which ingredient or ingredients cause the reaction you observe when you drop a seltzer tablet into water.

- Weigh out an amount of Alka-Seltzer or Bromo-Seltzer antacid that has the same weight as a single seltzer tablet. Add the antacid and the seltzer tablet to equal amounts of water in separate identical clear cups. Which sample do you think will react faster? Were you right?

CHAPTER 4

Energy in Chemical and Physical Changes

In Chapter 1, Experiments 1.7 and 1.8, you found that when substances melt or boil, the temperature remains constant. You may have wondered how this could happen when heat was being removed from or added to the substance. Normally, when we add heat to a substance, its temperature rises and its molecules move faster. When we take heat away, its temperature drops and its molecules move slower. At a certain temperature a substance may undergo a physical change; it will change its state. When a solid becomes a liquid or a liquid becomes a gas, it has changed its state.

◄ This photograph shows the solid (ice) and liquid (water) states of H_2O. Energy in the form of heat is needed to melt ice and change its state from solid to liquid.

During a change of state, energy is involved in changing the structure of the substance, but not in changing its temperature. In the case of melting, energy is needed to break the rigid bonds that hold the molecules in place. Breaking the bonds allows molecules to move freely around one another in the liquid state. The thermal (heat) energy added or removed does not change the average speed of the molecules.

To change a liquid to a gas during boiling, energy is needed to separate the molecules. As you know from experience, energy is required to lift a weight; that is, to separate it from the earth. Similarly, energy is required to separate molecules from one another. Just as objects are attracted to the earth by gravity, molecules are attracted to one another.

When a liquid freezes, the energy it gives up comes from the formation of rigid bonds between the molecules, not from a decrease in the average speed of its molecules. During condensation, the energy released comes from the loss of potential energy when the molecules come together, not from a loss in average molecular speed.

Energy must be added to melt ice or boil water. Energy is released when water freezes or when steam condenses. These are physical changes because no new substances are formed. As you will see in this chapter, energy is also involved in chemical changes, in which new substances are formed. But first you will investigate the energy required or released during physical changes (changes of state).

EXPERIMENT 4.1

The Energy (Heat) Needed to Melt Ice

Question:

Is there a relationship between the amount of heat needed to melt ice and the amount of heat released when ice melts?

Hypothesis:

The heat used to melt ice should equal the heat released when the same quantity of water freezes.

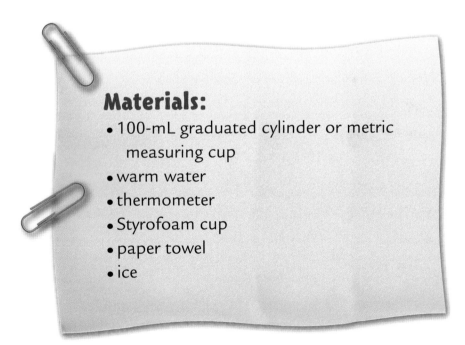

Materials:

- 100-mL graduated cylinder or metric measuring cup
- warm water
- thermometer
- Styrofoam cup
- paper towel
- ice

As you read earlier, energy (heat) must be added to change solid water (ice) to its liquid state. In this experiment, you'll try to find the amount of heat needed to melt one gram of ice. This quantity of heat is known as the heat of fusion.

Heat can be measured in calories. One calorie is the amount of heat gained (or lost) when one gram of water changes its temperature by one degree Celsius. If the temperature of 100 grams of water rose by 10°C, the heat transferred to the water would have been 1,000 calories (100 g × 10°C = 1,000 cal). If its temperature fell by 10°C, it would have transferred 1,000 calories to something else.

Procedure:

1. To begin the experiment, pour 100 mL (100 g) of warm (about 30°C) tap water into a Styrofoam cup. Use a paper towel to remove any cold water that may lie on the surface of a small ice cube.

2. Use the thermometer to stir the water and add the ice cube as shown in Figure 13. Continue to add small pieces of ice until the water reaches approximately 10°C.

   Cooling the water to a temperature as far below room temperature as it was above room temperature when you started will offset heat lost and gained to the air. The heat lost by the warm water to the cooler air as it cools from 30°C to 20°C during the first part of the experiment will balance the heat gained from the warmer air as the water cools from 20°C to 10°C.

3. Pour the water, which now contains the melted ice, into a graduated cylinder. How much ice melted?

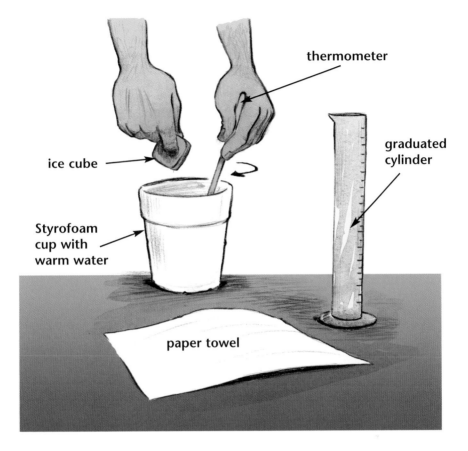

Figure 13.

The materials shown here can be used to find the heat of fusion for water.

Results and Conclusions

The heat lost by the warm water can be found from the weight of the water (100 g) and its change in temperature. In the example given, the change in temperature of the warm water was 20°C (30°C – 10°C).

Therefore, the warm water lost 2,000 calories because

$$100 \text{ g} \times 20°C = 2,000 \text{ cal}$$

However, in this experiment the heat lost by the water did two things: (1) It melted the ice. (2) It warmed the melted ice from 0°C to the final temperature of the water (10°C).

In the example given, suppose the final volume of water was 122 mL. Since 22 g of ice melted (122 g – 100 g), the heat required to warm the melted ice from 0° to 10°C was 220 cal (22 g × 10°C). The remaining 1780 calories (2,000 – 220) was the heat used to melt the ice. According to this example, the heat needed to melt one gram of ice (the heat of fusion) was

$$1780 \text{ cal} \div 22 \text{ g} = 81 \text{ cal/g}$$

How does this value compare with the one you found in your experiment?

Millions of experiments have shown that energy, like matter, is conserved. That is, energy is never created or destroyed. We know, then, that the heat used to melt one gram of ice will equal the heat released when one gram of water freezes.

Science Project Ideas

- Does the shape of a piece of ice affect the rate at which it melts? Design and conduct an experiment to find out. Can you explain your results?

- You may have seen icicles form when snow melts and drips off a roof. How can water freeze to form icicles when the temperature is warm enough to melt the snow?

EXPERIMENT 4.2

The Energy (Heat) Needed to Boil Water

Question:

How can you find how much energy is needed to boil a certain quantity of water?

Hypothesis:

We can calculate the energy if you know the heating power of the heat source, the water's starting temperature, and the amount of time required to bring the water to a boil.

Materials:

- **an adult**
- 2 pairs of safety goggles, long-sleeved shirts, and oven mitts
- 200-watt electric immersion heater
- electrical outlet
- graduated cylinder or metric measuring cup
- beaker or can
- 12- or 14-oz Styrofoam cups
- water
- thermometer with a range of −10°C to 110°C
- watch with second hand
- notebook and pencil

Safety: *Work* **under adult supervision** *during this experiment because you'll be using electricity and very hot water. Wear goggles, a long-sleeved shirt, and oven mitts throughout this experiment.*

The boiling point of water at sea level is approximately 100°C. You have seen that water temperature remains at the boiling point for as long as the water boils. The energy added to the boiling water does not increase the water's temperature. That energy is used to separate the molecules of water from each other.

The heat needed to change one gram of a liquid at its boiling point to a gas is called the heat of vaporization. A rough estimate of the heat of vaporization for water can be done by using a 200-watt electric immersion heater. **Safety:** *An immersion heater should never be plugged into an electrical outlet unless its coil is in water!*

Although a label on an immersion heater may read 200 W, the actual power of the heater may be somewhat higher or lower. Consequently, the first thing you should do is calibrate the heater. That is, find out how much heat the heater provides in one minute.

Procedure:

1. Put 200 grams of cold water in a 12- or 14-oz Styrofoam cup. (Stacking two or three such cups together will provide better insulation. Place the cups in a beaker or can to provide additional support.)

   If possible, use water that is 5° to 10°C cooler than the room. This will reduce heat losses that occur when the water temperature rises above room temperature.

2. Place the immersion heater in the cold water. Use a thermometer to measure the water temperature (see Figure 14). After recording the initial temperature of the water, record the exact time **the adult** plugs the immersion heater into an electrical outlet.

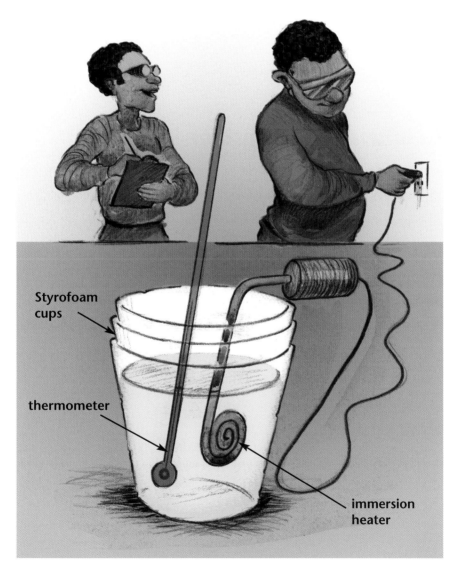

Styrofoam cups

thermometer

immersion heater

Figure 14.

An immersion heater can be used to heat water and obtain an estimate of the heat of vaporization for water.

3. Stir the water gently with the thermometer as the water is heated. After exactly one minute, **ask the adult** to remove the plug (grasping the plug, not the cord) from the outlet to disconnect the heater. Leave the heater in the cup as you stir the water to find its final temperature. Why should you leave the heater in the water after it is disconnected?

4. Record the final temperature of the water. By how many degrees did the water's temperature change?

Results and Conclusions

Use the data you have collected to calculate how much heat, in calories, the immersion heater transferred to the water in one minute.

Repeat the experiment several times to be sure your results are consistent. How much heat does the immersion heater deliver in one minute? How much heat do you predict it will deliver in 30 seconds? Test your prediction. Were you right?

If the heater really delivers as much heat per second as its rating (200 W) indicates, it provides 2,870 calories per minute. How does this value compare with the value you found by experiment?

Procedure:

1. Now place 150 ml (150 g) of cold tap water in a stack of two or three insulated Styrofoam cups supported by a beaker or can. With only 150 g of water, very little will spatter from the cup when the water boils.

2. Put the cooled immersion heater in the water, stir, and record the initial temperature of the water.

3. **Ask the adult** to plug in the heater, note the time, and let it transfer heat to the water for 7 or 8 minutes.

4. During that period of time, a significant amount of water should boil away. Once the water is boiling, record its temperature. Why might it boil at some temperature other than 100°C?

5. **Ask the adult** to disconnect the heater while you record the total time you have added heat to the water. Then remove the heater from the water.

6. **Ask the adult**, who should be wearing oven mitts and safety goggles, to pour the hot water into a graduated cylinder. How much water remains? What mass of water was changed to gas?

Results and Conclusions

With the data you have collected, you can make a reasonable estimate of the amount of heat required to boil away one gram of water at its boiling point. For example, suppose that your heater transfers 3,000 cal/min. In 8 minutes it will provide 24,000 cal. If the initial temperature of the water was 20°C and the boiling temperature was 100°C, then 12,000 calories (150 g × 80°C) were required to bring the water to the boiling point. Assume that the remaining 12,000 calories (24,000 − 12,000) were used to change liquid water to gaseous water. If 20 g of water boiled away, then the energy required to boil away one gram of water was

$$12,000 \text{ cal} \div 20 \text{ g} = 600 \text{ cal/g}$$

Using your data, what do you find is the heat of vaporization for water?

Examine the heats of fusion and vaporization for the substances listed in Table 4. How do your estimates for the heats of fusion and vaporization for water compare with the values given in the table? How do the heats of fusion and vaporization for water compare with those of other substances that have about the same molecular or atomic weight?

Table 4.

Molecular Weight, in Atomic Mass Units (AMU), and Heats of Vaporization and Fusion for a Few Substances with Molecular Weights Reasonably Close to Water's (18).

Substance	Molecular or atomic weight (amu)	Heat of vaporization (cal/g)	Heat of fusion (cal/g)
Aluminum	27	2,500	95
Ammonia	17	329	108
Copper	63.5	1,150	49
Ethanol	46	205	26
Hydrogen	2	108	14
Oxygen	32	51	3
Sulfur dioxide	64	95	24
Water	18	540	80

EXPERIMENT 4.3

The Heat of Condensation

Question:

Can you calculate the amount of energy released when steam condenses?

Hypothesis:

You can make the calculation if you know the amount of water produced when the steam condenses and the number of degrees lost from the water's boiling point.

Materials:

- **an adult**
- 2 pairs of safety goggles and oven mitts
- ring stand and clamp
- large test tube (25 x 150 mm)
- water
- boiling chips (calcium carbonate)
- one-hole rubber stopper that fits test tube
- short length of rubber tubing
- right-angle glass bend
- glass eyedropper
- Bunsen burner or alcohol burner
- scissors
- 6- or 7-oz Styrofoam cup
- balance that can weigh to nearest 0.1 gram or better
- notebook and pencil
- thermometer
- graduated cylinder or metric measuring cup

When an object moves farther from the Earth, the Earth's pull of gravity on the object is lessened. Its speed and kinetic (motion) energy decreases. As a result, because energy is conserved, the object's gravitational potential energy increases. The raised object can transfer its potential energy to another object as it falls back to Earth. That energy can be used to do work—to pump water, for instance.

In a similar way, molecules of water acquire potential energy when they are separated from each other. So it is not surprising that heat is released when gaseous water molecules come back together (condense) to form a liquid.

In the previous experiment, you measured the quantity of energy needed to boil away one gram of water. The law of conservation of energy would suggest that the same quantity of energy would be released when one gram of steam condenses back to liquid water.

To find out if this is so, you can let some steam condense in cold water. Is energy released when this happens? If it is, is the amount of energy per gram released similar to the energy per gram absorbed when water boils?

Safety: *Since steam can cause severe burns, an adult should do parts of this experiment.*

Procedure:

1. Set up the apparatus as shown in Figure 15.

2. Fill the large test tube about one third of the way with water. Add several boiling chips (pieces of calcium carbonate) to prevent violent boiling that might cause water to leave the test tube.

3. Put a one-hole rubber stopper fitted with a right-angle glass bend in the mouth of the test tube. Add a short length of rubber tubing in order to connect the glass bend to a glass eyedropper that has a narrow opening. **Under adult supervision**, heat the water with a Bunsen burner or an alcohol burner, being ready to move the burner so as not to force water out of the test tube. The idea is to send steam, not boiling water, from the test tube.

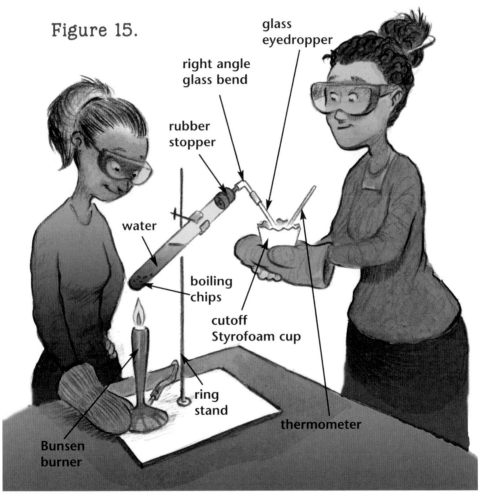

Figure 15.

glass eyedropper

right angle glass bend

rubber stopper

water

boiling chips

cutoff Styrofoam cup

ring stand

thermometer

Bunsen burner

A steam generator will produce gaseous water. The gas will condense in cold water, enabling you to find a value for the heat of condensation for water.

Steam produced in the large test tube will flow through the right-angle glass bend and eyedropper into the cold water. There it will condense.

6. Using scissors, cut away the top third of a 6- or 7-oz Styrofoam cup.

7. **Have the adult** begin heating the water in the test tube while you weigh and record the weight of the cutoff cup. Add about 100 mL of cold water to the cup. That water should be about 10°C below room temperature.

8. Weigh the cup and the water. What is the weight of the cold water?

9. When steam without water droplets is coming from the eyedropper, use the thermometer to measure the exact temperature of the cold water. Record this temperature.

10. **The adult**, with safety goggles and oven mitts on, should hold the cup of cold water so that the end of the eyedropper is beneath the water's surface. You'll hear the steam sputter as it condenses in the cold water. Stir the water gently with the thermometer.

11. When the water temperature reaches a temperature about 10°C greater than room temperature, remove the cup from the steam. Stir and record the water's maximum temperature.

    Safety: *The adult should turn off the burner while you determine the mass of the cup, water, and condensed steam.*

Results and Conclusions

What mass of steam condensed? Why is it a good procedure to start with water colder than the room and allow its temperature to rise to a level warmer than the room?

How much heat, in calories, was transferred to the cold water? How much heat was released by the steam as it condensed? Don't forget to subtract the heat that came from the hot water after it condensed. For example, if 3.5 g of steam condensed and the final temperature of the water was 30°C, then 3.5 g of condensed steam gave up 245 calories in cooling from 100°C down to 30°C (3.5 g × 70°C).

What is the heat of condensation for water (heat per gram of water condensed) according to your data? That is, how much heat is released when one gram of water vapor condenses to liquid at the boiling point? Is this value similar to that of the heat of vaporization?

In the example above, the 3.5 g of steam raised the temperature of the cold water by 20°C. It provided 2,000 calories to the cold water (100 g × 20°C = 2,000 cal). Of that 2,000 calories, 245 calories came from the steam after it condensed. Therefore, the heat due to condensation was 1,755 calories (2,000 − 245). The heat released per gram of steam condensed would be 501 cal/g (1,755 cal ÷ 3.5 g = 501 cal/g).

Examine the heats of fusion and vaporization for the substances listed in Table 4. How does the energy required to separate the atoms of a metal compare with that required to separate the molecules of liquids? How does the heat of vaporization for water compare with that of other liquids and gases whose molecules have a similar weight? How might you explain water's rather extraordinary heat of vaporization?

EXPERIMENT 4.4

Energy Changes During Physical and Chemical Changes

Question:

When one substance dissolves into another, is there a loss or gain of energy during the process?

Hypothesis:

In some instances energy is released and in others energy is absorbed.

Materials:

- **an adult**
- sink
- water
- Epsom salt
- small glass or test tube
- thermometer
- teaspoon
- ammonium chloride
- sodium hydroxide
- scoopula or spatula

- 2 pairs of safety goggles and oven mitts
- graduated cylinder or metric measuring cup
- 3% solution of hydrogen peroxide
- 12-oz Styrofoam cup
- tablespoon
- dry yeast

There are changes in energy when solid substances dissolve in water.

Some substances, such as salts, are made up of ions (charged atoms).

Ordinary salt, such as sodium chloride, consists of sodium ions (Na^+)

and chloride ions (Cl$^-$). Separating the molecules or ions of the solids requires an input of energy. However, the attraction between water molecules and the molecules or ions in the solid can change potential energy to kinetic energy (motion). The kinetic energy appears as an increase in the speed of the particles. This causes an increase in temperature, because temperature rises in proportion to the average kinetic energy of the molecules. When energy is released and the temperature rises, we say the dissolving is exothermic. If energy is absorbed, the temperature decreases, and we say the dissolving is endothermic.

You can test a number of substances to see whether they absorb or release energy when they dissolve. **Safety:** *After testing each one, pour the solution into a sink and flush it down the drain with plenty of water.*

Procedure:

1. To find out what happens when Epsom salt dissolves in water, pour some water into a small glass or test tube. Use a thermometer to find the temperature of the water. (It should be approximately room temperature.)

3. Add one teaspoon of Epsom salt (magnesium sulfate) and stir. What happens to the temperature of the mixture? Is the dissolving of Epsom salt exothermic or endothermic?

4. Repeat the experiment using ammonium chloride (NH_4Cl). Is the dissolving of ammonium chloride exothermic or endothermic?

5. Add about 20 mL of water to a test tube or small glass.

6. **Ask an adult** to use a scoopula or spatula to add a few pellets of sodium hydroxide (NaOH) to the water. Sodium hydroxide should never touch skin. It is very corrosive. Therefore, **the adult** should wear safety goggles and oven mitts when handling sodium hydroxide. Should any of the solid touch skin, the skin should be rinsed with cold water immediately.

7. Stir the mixture with your thermometer. Is the dissolving of sodium hydroxide exothermic or endothermic? **The adult** can dispose of the solution by pouring it into a sink drain with plenty of cold water.

Results and Conclusions

Chemical changes can also be exothermic or endothermic. For example, when an electric current is passed through water (H_2O), the water breaks down into oxygen (O_2) and hydrogen (H_2). It is an endothermic reaction because electrical energy is absorbed in the process and stored as chemical energy in the gases.

Procedure:

1. Add about 60 mL of a 3% hydrogen peroxide solution to a 12-oz Styrofoam cup.

2. Place a thermometer into the liquid. Record the temperature of the hydrogen peroxide solution and remove the thermometer. Then pour one tablespoon of dry yeast into the solution.

Results and Conclusions

As you saw in Experiment 3.4, hydrogen peroxide (H_2O_2) slowly changes to water and oxygen. You also saw how a catalyst can affect the rate of the reaction. In this experiment you'll see that yeast can also serve as a catalyst for the decomposition of hydrogen peroxide. You'll also discover that there are changes in energy. What happens in the cup? What gas do you think is being produced? How could you determine whether you are right?

Put the thermometer back in the liquid. What has happened to the temperature? Is the decomposition of hydrogen peroxide an exothermic or an endothermic reaction?

EXPERIMENT 4.5

A Chemical Reaction: Reactants, Products, and Energy Changes

Question:

How does lighting a common candle illustrate one of the most fundamental and important chemical reactions of all?

Hypothesis:

A burning candle is a chemical reaction that causes the reactants—wax and oxygen—to change. They also release heat and carbon dioxide.

Materials:

- **an adult**
- matches
- short candle
- aluminum can lid
- 1-L beaker or quart jar
- cobalt chloride paper
- two 250-mL Erlenmeyer flasks
- limewater
- straw
- balance
- paper punch
- 6-oz frozen juice can
- stick, glass rod, or long nail
- ring and ring stand
- graduated cylinder or metric measuring cup
- cold water
- thermometer
- notebook and pencil

Safety: *Because you'll be using a candle flame in this experiment, you should work with an adult.*

When a chemical reaction takes place, substances that change during it are called reactants. Substances that form during the reaction are called products.

In this experiment, you'll try to identify the reactants and products of a chemical reaction. You'll also measure the heat released. The reaction is a very common one—the burning of a candle.

Procedure:

1. To prepare for the experiment, **with an adult's help** light a short candle.

2. Once the candle is burning smoothly, tip it so that some wax falls onto an aluminum can lid. Before the wax solidifies, place the candle on the wax. When the wax solidifies, it will keep the candle upright and in place. (See Figure 16.)

Results and Conclusions

As you know, when a candle burns, the wax burns away and heat is released. Candle wax generally consists of 60 percent paraffin, 35 percent stearic acid, and 5 percent beeswax. These materials consist of large molecules that contain mostly carbon and hydrogen. Paraffin is a white solid consisting of a mixture of high-molecular-weight hydrocarbons (compounds that contain only carbon and hydrogen). The formula for stearic acid is $C_{18}H_{36}O_2$. Beeswax is a mixture of compounds consisting mostly of hydrogen and carbon and small amounts of oxygen.

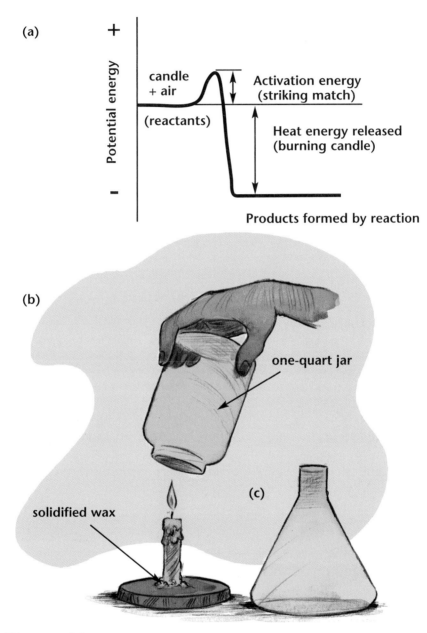

Figure 16.

a) To make a candle start to burn, some energy must be provided. This is called the activation energy. Once the reaction starts, potential energy is released as the candle burns.
b) What happens if you restrict the amount of air available to the candle?
c) Use an Erlenmeyer flask to cover the candle.

For a candle to burn, it must be in contact with air. As you found earlier, the component of air that is essential for combustion is oxygen. Therefore, we know that when a candle burns, the reactants (the substances that combine) are wax and oxygen.

As in many chemical reactions, a certain amount of energy—the activation energy—must be supplied to start the reaction. In the case of a burning candle, the flame on a match provides enough energy to start the reaction. Once it begins, the reaction is exothermic. The burning candle releases energy in the form of heat. The energy changes involved are shown in Figure 16a. The potential energy stored in the candle and oxygen is released as heat energy once the activation energy is provided.

What happens if the air supply is limited?

Procedure:

1. To find out, reduce a candle's air supply by placing a 1-L beaker or a quart jar over the candle as shown in Figure 16b. What happens?

   As you can see, a thin film of liquid has condensed on the glass that covered the candle.

2. To see if it might be water, you can hold a piece of cobalt chloride paper against the liquid. Cobalt chloride, which is blue when dehydrated, turns pink when water is added. Is the liquid water? Could it be something else?

3. **Ask an adult** to light the candle again.

4. When the candle is burning smoothly, place a 250-mL Erlenmeyer flask beside the candle (see Figure 16c). Then invert a second 250-mL Erlenmeyer flask over the candle.

5. After the flame goes out, remove the second flask and place it beside the first one.

6. Add 20 mL of limewater to both flasks and swirl them.

Results and Conclusions

Limewater turns milky when in the presence of carbon dioxide (CO_2). Does the limewater in either flask turn milky? What can you conclude?

As you probably know, there is carbon dioxide in the air you exhale. What do you think will happen if you use a straw to blow your lung air into the limewater in the flask that didn't become milky? Try it! Was your prediction correct?

Based on your observations, what are two likely products of the reaction between candle wax and oxygen?

There are two possible reasons why the candle went out when the flask was covering it. One or more of the reactants was in limited supply, or one or more of the products, when not removed, stopped the reaction. Why do you think the candle went out when it was covered by a glass vessel?

Energy Changes

Procedure:

1. To find out how much energy is released per gram of wax burned, you should first weigh a short candle that is fixed to an aluminum can lid. Record the weight.

2. Next, use a paper punch to make two holes, opposite one another, near the top of an empty 6-oz frozen juice can. (The can should have a metal base and cardboard sides.)

3. Put a stick, glass rod, or long nail though the holes to support the can on a ring connected to a ring stand as shown in Figure 17.

4. Place the candle under the can.

5. Add 100 mL of cold water (10°C to 15°C below room temperature) to the can and **ask an adult** to light the candle. The top of the flame should just touch the bottom of the can.

6. Stir the water with the thermometer. When the temperature of the water is 10°C to 15°C above room temperature, blow out the candle.

7. Record the final temperature of the water and reweigh the candle and lid.

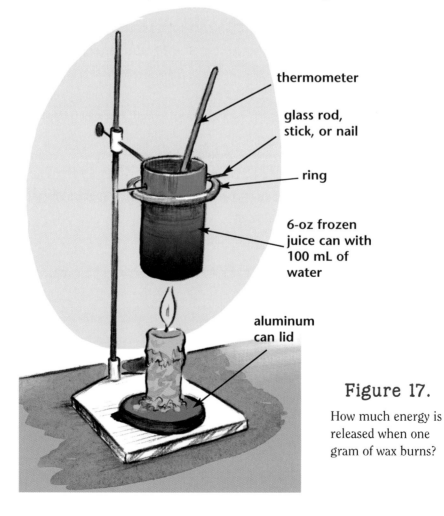

thermometer

glass rod,
stick, or nail

ring

6-oz frozen
juice can with
100 mL of
water

aluminum
can lid

Figure 17.

How much energy is released when one gram of wax burns?

Results and Conclusions

How much heat, in calories, did the candle transfer to the water? How much weight did the candle lose? Based on your data, how much heat per gram of wax burned is released by the reaction between candle wax and oxygen?

💡 Science Project Ideas

- In Experiment 4.5 some of the heat released as the candle burned was not transferred to the water. It was used to warm surrounding air. Design a way to do this experiment that would reduce heat losses to the surroundings. Then, **under adult supervision,** carry out the experiment. How much heat per gram of wax burned is produced in this reaction when you use your modified experiment? How does it compare with the value you found before?

- Does the heat per gram of wax burned depend on the kind of candle you burn? Design an experiment to find out. Then, **under adult supervision,** carry out your experiment.

- Design an experiment to measure the energy stored in a peanut. Then carry out the experiment **under adult supervision.**

CHAPTER 5

Acids, Bases, Ions, and an Electric Cell

E arly in the history of chemistry, chemists discovered that molten (melted) salts, such as sodium chloride (NaCl) or potassium iodide (KI), would conduct electricity. To explain this behavior, a young Swedish chemist named Svante Arrhenius proposed in 1884 that such salts consisted of ions. As you saw in the last chapter, ions are atoms that carry an electric charge. You may know that electric charges flow between positive and negative electrodes connected to a battery. Ions, Arrenhius proposed, carry charge from one electrode to the other. In the case of sodium chloride, the salt is made up of positive sodium ions (Na^+)

◀ Jumper cables can conduct electric charges to or from automotive batteries. These batteries usually contain lead and lead-oxide plates in a sulfuric acid solution.

and negative chloride ions (Cl^-). When an electric current is passed through molten sodium chloride, sodium metal collects at the negative electrode and chlorine gas bubbles off the positive electrode.

Most chemists did not accept Arrhenius's theory. However, when J. J. Thomson discovered the electron (an elementary particle with a negative charge) in 1897, and certain elements, such as uranium, were found to give off charged particles (radiation), Arrhenius's idea became widely accepted. It became clear that atoms contained charged particles—electrons and protons. A chloride ion was an atom that had one extra electron, while on the other hand a sodium ion was an atom that had lost one electron. In recognition of his work, Arrhenius was awarded the Nobel prize for chemistry in 1903.

EXPERIMENT 5.1

Ions and Electric Current

Question:
Do all substances conduct electricity?

Hypothesis:
Substances without ions do not conduct electricity.

Materials:
- table salt
- clear plastic vial
- 6-volt dry-cell battery or 4 D–cell batteries, masking tape, and a mailing tube
- flashlight bulb and socket
- insulated wires with alligator clips
- paper clips
- water
- coffee stirrer or swizzle stick
- Epsom salt
- sugar

When you hear the word *salt*, you probably think of the white crystals you shake onto food to add flavor. To a chemist, however, a salt is a compound that consists of positive and negative ions. For example, ordinary table salt, sodium chloride, consists of equal numbers of positive sodium ions (Na^+)

and negative chloride ions (Cl^-). Calcium chloride ($CaCl_2$) has two singly charged chloride ions (Cl^-) for every one doubly charged calcium ion (Ca^{+2}). Aluminum ions carry an excess of three positive charges (Al^{+3}). What would be the chemical formula for aluminum chloride?

Will ordinary solid salt, the kind you put on food, conduct electricity?

Procedure:

1. Nearly fill a clear plastic vial with table salt.

2. Add two paper clips as shown in Figure 18a, then connect them to a 6-volt dry-cell battery through a flashlight bulb in a socket. If you do not have such a battery, you can make one by placing four D–cell batteries head to tail (Figure 18a) in a mailing tube. The tube should be slightly shorter than the total length of the four D cells. Use masking tape to fasten paper clips firmly against the positive and negative terminals, as shown.

3. Insulated wires with alligator clips can be used to connect the 4-D-cell battery to a flashlight bulb in a socket (holder) and to the paper clips on each side of the vial of salt, as shown in Figure 18a. If you do not have a bulb socket, touch the metal base of the bulb with one wire and the metal side with a second wire, as shown in Figure 18b. If you do not have wires with alligator clips, you can use clothespins to hold the ends of the wires in place.

Results and Conclusions

Does the bulb light? Does solid table salt conduct electricity? Suppose you dissolve some of the salt in water. Do you think the solution will conduct electricity?

Figure 18.

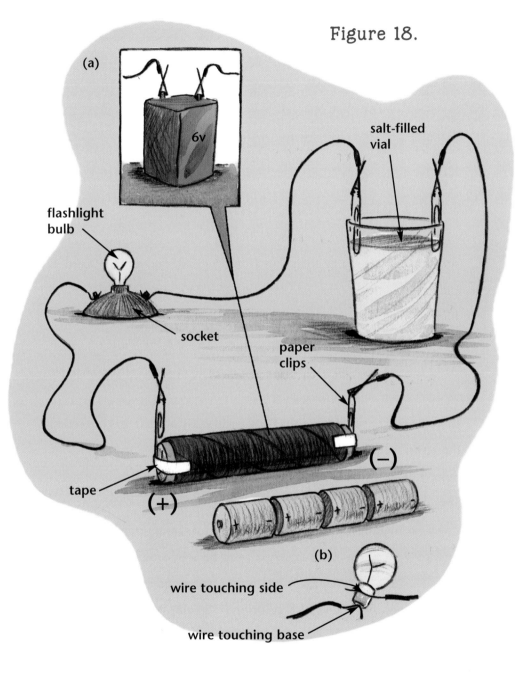

(a)

6v

flashlight
bulb

salt-filled
vial

socket

paper
clips

tape

(−)

(+)

(b)

wire touching side

wire touching base

The apparatus shown can be used to test the electrical
conductivity of salt, solutions of salt, and a sugar solution.

Procedure:

1. Remove half of the solid salt from the vial, add water to nearly fill it, and stir with a coffee stirrer to dissolve as much of the salt as possible.

2. Connect the paper clips on the vial to the battery and a light bulb, as shown in Figure 18.

Results and Conclusions

Does the bulb light now? What does this tell you?

You won't find sodium collecting at the negative electrode. If it did, it would react with water to release hydrogen. The chemical reaction of sodium with water is

$$2Na + 2H_2O \longrightarrow H_2 + 2Na^+ + 2OH^-$$

What do you see that indicates a gas is being released at the negative electrode? What might that gas be?

Chlorine is very soluble in water. Why will you not see a gas collecting at the positive electrode?

Epsom salt, so named because it was first obtained from mineral springs in Epsom, England, is magnesium sulfate. It is used as a purgative and for making solutions to bathe painful joints. Magnesium sulfate ($MgSO_4$) crystals contain equal numbers of magnesium (Mg^{+2}) and sulfate (SO_4^{-2}) ions. Each of these ions carries an excess of two electric charges. Do you think a solution of Epsom salt will conduct an electric current?

Procedure:

1. Fill the vial you used before about halfway with Epsom salt.

2. Add water until the vial is nearly full and stir.

3. Connect the vial's paper clip electrodes to the 6-volt battery through the light bulb.

Results and Conclusions

Does the flashlight bulb glow? Did you predict the result?

What about substances that do not have ions, such as sugar? The molecular formula for ordinary table sugar, whose chemical name is sucrose, is $C_{12}H_{22}O_{11}$. Do you think it will conduct electricity when dissolved in water?

Procedure:

1. Fill the vial you used about halfway with sugar. Add water until the vial is nearly full. Stir to make a solution of sugar.

2. Connect the paper clip electrodes to the battery and light bulb.

Results and Conclusions

Does the sugar solution conduct electricity? Was your prediction correct?

Many chemicals can be identified as acids or bases. Substances that are neither acidic nor basic, such as water, are said to be neutral. The Latin word for acid, *acidus*, means "sharp" or "sour," so sour-tasting substances came to be known as acids. In addition to their sour taste, acids dissolve in water to form solutions that conduct electricity; they contain hydrogen that is released when the acid is added to certain metals such as zinc; they turn blue litmus paper red; and they neutralize bases—that is, they combine with bases to form a substance that is neither an acid nor a base.

Bases are also called alkalis, a word that means "ashes." Ashes have properties that chemists use to identify bases. They have a bitter taste and feel slippery like soap. American pioneers made soap by boiling wood ashes with animal fat. Bases, like acids, are conductors of electricity. They turn red litmus paper blue and neutralize acids.

Acids and bases conduct electricity because they form ions when dissolved in water. Acids form hydrogen ions (H^+) and bases form hydroxide ions (OH^-). The chemical equation below shows how acids and bases neutralize one another to form water (HOH, or H_2O).

$$H^+ + OH^- \longrightarrow HOH, \text{ or } H_2O$$

If the acid is hydrochloric acid, HCl, and the base is sodium hydroxide, NaOH, then the overall reaction is

$$H^+ + Cl^- + Na^+ + OH^- \longrightarrow H_2O + Na^+ + Cl^-$$

If the water is allowed to evaporate after the reaction, crystals of salt (sodium chloride, NaCl) will be seen.

EXPERIMENT 5.2

Identifying Acids and Bases

Question:

Are there natural methods to find whether a substance is an acid or a base?

Hypothesis:

Certain natural juices and extracts work well as simple indicators of acidity and basicity.

Materials:

- **an adult**
- lemon juice
- red and blue litmus paper (obtain from a science teacher or a science supply company)
- blackberries
- substances for testing: apple juice, grapefruit juice, rubbing alcohol, powdered cleanser, salt and sugar solutions, aspirin, wood ashes, baking soda, baking powder, lime (calcium oxide), citric acid or Kool-Aid or Tang drink mix crystals, milk of magnesia, washing soda, ginger ale, tonic water, seltzer water, pickle juice, olive juice
- fork

(continued)

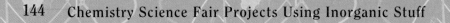

(continued)

- bowl
- strainer
- cups or glasses
- red cabbage
- non-aluminum pot and cover
- water
- stove
- tongs
- container with lid
- refrigerator
- white vinegar
- glass jars or test tubes
- eyedropper
- household ammonia

Procedure:

1. Place a drop of lemon juice on your tongue. Do you think lemon juice is an acid or a base? Why?

2. To test your hypothesis about lemon juice, dip pieces of red and blue litmus paper into the liquid. What do you find?

    Litmus paper is not the only way to test for acids and bases. There are many acid-base indicators. You can easily make your own.

3. Put five or six blackberries in a bowl. Crush them thoroughly with a fork until you have something resembling blackberry jam. Then pour the "jam" into a strainer and collect the dark red juice in a cup or a glass. Save any juice you do not use here. You will use it in the next experiment to make indicator sticks.

    You can also use red cabbage juice as an acid-base indicator.

4. Remove a few leaves from a red cabbage. Break the leaves into small pieces and place them in a non-aluminum pot together with enough water to just cover the leaves.

5. Put a cover on the pot and **ask an adult** to help you heat the pot on a stove until the water is boiling. Reduce the heat, but continue boiling for about half an hour. Then turn off the heat and let the water cool to room temperature.

6. Using tongs, remove the cabbage leaves. Pour the cabbage juice solution into a container.

7. Cover it and put it in a refrigerator.

Vinegar is a solution of acetic acid ($C_2H_4O_2$), which, as you probably know, has a sour taste.

8. To confirm that vinegar is an acid, dip a piece of blue litmus paper into a few milliliters of white vinegar. How does this help you identify vinegar as an acid?

9. Now add a few drops of the cabbage extract to the white vinegar in a small glass jar or test tube. What is the color of the cabbage juice indicator in an acid?

When ammonia gas (NH_3) dissolves in water, some of it reacts with the water to form ammonium (NH_4^+) and hydroxide ions (OH^-), as shown by the chemical equation below:

$$NH_3 + H_2O \longrightarrow NH_4^+ + OH^-$$

10. To confirm that an ammonia solution is basic, dip a piece of red litmus paper into a few milliliters of a household ammonia solution. How can you tell that the ammonia solution is a base?

11. Next, add a few drops of the cabbage juice to a few milliliters of ammonia. What is the color of the cabbage juice indicator in a base?

12. Add a few drops of the indicator to some tap water. What is the color of the indicator in a neutral solution?

13. Repeat the experiment using the berry juice extract. What is the color of the berry juice indicator in an acid? What is the color of the berry juice indicator in a base? In a neutral solution?

14. Using litmus paper, berry juice, and cabbage juice, test the following substances to determine whether each is an acid, a base, or neutral: lemon juice, apple juice, grapefruit juice, rubbing alcohol, powdered cleanser (in water), salt and sugar solutions, crushed aspirin dissolved in water, wood ashes mixed with water, solutions of baking soda and baking powder, lime (calcium oxide) in water, citric acid or Kool-Aid or Tang drink mix crystals dissolved in water, milk of magnesia, washing soda dissolved in water, ginger ale, tonic water, seltzer water, pickle juice, and the juice from a jar of olives.

Results and Conclusions

Which of these substances are acids? Which are bases? Which are neutral? Which natural indicator juice, berry or cabbage, do you prefer? Why do you prefer one over the other?

💡 Science Project Ideas

- Turmeric, a common spice, can also be used as an acid-base indicator. Prepare an extract of turmeric by mixing ¼ teaspoon of turmeric with a ¼ cup of rubbing alcohol. Add a few drops of the turmeric indicator to acids, bases, and neutral substances. How does it compare with other indicators you have tried?

- Investigate other common indicators that can be found in many science rooms or obtained from a science supply company. These include phenolphthalein, methyl orange, methyl red, bromthymol blue, congo red, indigo carmine, and alizarin yellow. Other than color, how do they differ?

- Read the label on a bottle of vitamin C tablets. Crush one of the tablets into a powder and dissolve it in water. (Depending on the type of tablet, the mixture may be cloudy because some of the ingredients may not be soluble.) Divide the solution into three parts. Predict the color of litmus paper, drops of cabbage juice, and drops of berry juice when added to a solution of vitamin C.

- Prepare a cup of hot tea. Then add a few drops of lemon juice to the tea. What evidence do you have to suggest that tea is an acid-base indicator?

EXPERIMENT 5.3

Indicator Papers and Sticks

Question:

Can we make natural indicator papers to test for acids and bases?

Hypothesis:

Indicator papers similar to litmus paper can be prepared using berry and cabbage extracts.

Materials:

- scissors
- ruler
- white construction paper, coffee filters, or filter paper
- berry and cabbage extracts from previous experiments
- paper towels
- extra containers
- vinegar
- ammonia
- substances for testing: lemon juice, apple juice, grapefruit juice, rubbing alcohol, powdered cleanser, salt and sugar solutions, aspirin, wood ashes, baking soda, baking powder, lime (calcium oxide), citric acid or Kool-Aid or Tang drink mix crystals, milk of magnesia, washing soda, ginger ale, tonic water, seltzer water, pickle juice, olive juice

You can prepare indicator papers similar to litmus paper using the berry and cabbage extracts you prepared in the previous experiment.

Procedure:

1. Use scissors to cut rectangular strips about 5 cm (2 in) long and 1 cm (½ in) wide from white construction paper, coffee filters, or filter paper.

2. Dip the strips in the berry or cabbage extracts and place them on paper towels to dry. Be sure to keep the two types of indicator papers separate.

3. If you prefer, you can divide each of your two indicator papers to give them two different colors, like litmus paper. Divide the berry and cabbage extracts in half.

4. Add a few drops of vinegar to half of the cabbage extract. This will color the cabbage juice red and give you red strips when you dip the papers into it.

5. To the second half of the cabbage extract, add a few drops of ammonia. This will turn the cabbage juice green and give you green strips when you dip the papers into it. Repeat the process for the berry juice and you will have two sets of paper strips for each indicator. You can use them just as you use red and blue litmus paper.

6. Use your cabbage and berry extract paper indicators to test the same substances you tested in the previous experiment.

Results and Conclusions

If you could use only one natural indicator, which one would you choose? Why? Do you prefer paper strips or drops as indicators? Why?

EXPERIMENT 5.4

Neutralization

Question:

Can acids and bases neutralize each other?

Hypothesis:

We can add an acid to a base or a base to an acid to see the neutralization process.

Materials:

- teaspoon
- milk of magnesia
- saucer
- water
- cabbage juice extract from Experiment 5.2
- eyedropper
- lemon juice
- sink

Procedure:

1. Pour about ½ teaspoon of milk of magnesia [$Mg(OH)_2$] into a saucer. Add about two teaspoons of water and stir.

2. Add several drops of the cabbage juice extract from Experiment 5.2 and stir the mixture to obtain a uniform color.

3. Using an eyedropper, add lemon juice (citric acid) drop by drop.

   Observe the color of the solution at the place where the drops of acid land. Stir the liquid as you add the drops until you see a distinct color change. What has happened?

4. Now go the other way. Rinse your eyedropper and use it to add drops of milk of magnesia to the solution.

Results and Conclusions

Do this slowly. Notice the effect of one drop on the color of the solution. Can you see an intermediate color (purple) just before the solution changes from acid to base or base to acid? Remember, cabbage juice is purple in a neutral substance. If you can see the indicator turn purple, you are witnessing the exact point at which neutralization occurs.

What happens to the color of the neutral solution if you add a drop or two of lemon juice? A drop or two of milk of magnesia?

 Science Project Idea

- Antacids, which come as tablets or liquids, are used to neutralize stomach acid. Design and carry out, **under adult supervision,** an experiment to test various antacids for their capacity to neutralize acids. Based on the ingredients in the antacid, try to determine how the antacid neutralizes the acid.

EXPERIMENT 5.5

Building an Electric Cell

Question:
How is an electric cell made?

Hypothesis:
A working electric cell can be easily constructed using common chemicals and materials found in a school science lab.

Materials:
All these materials are generally found in a school science room or lab.

- copper and zinc plates about 3.5 cm × 10 cm (1.5 in × 4 in)
- steel wool
- 2 drinking glasses or 250-mL beakers
- zinc nitrate solution: dissolve 29 g of zinc nitrate [$Zn(NO_3)_2 \cdot 6H_2O$] in 200 mL of distilled water

- copper nitrate solution: dissolve 24 g of copper nitrate [$Cu(NO_3)_2 \cdot 3H_2O$] in 200 mL of distilled water
- ammeter (0–5 amps)
- insulated wires with alligator clips
- paper towels
- voltmeter (0–3 volts)

Electricity from Chemicals

Until Michael Faraday discovered that electricity could be generated by changing the magnetic field through a coil of wire, all electricity came from batteries. We still use batteries, but batteries cannot provide the large amounts of power needed to operate most household appliances. On the other hand, flashlights, personal audio players, and pocket radios are useless without batteries. All automobiles have battery-powered electrical systems, and electric cars are powered by batteries rather than using gasoline. However, the batteries in such cars have to be connected to an electrical outlet frequently for recharging. Hybrid cars are powered by both gasoline and batteries. The batteries in hybrid cars are charged by generators that are activated when the car brakes or decelerates.

Batteries, such as those in cars, consist of two or more electric cells. Electric cells have one thing in common: They are all made from chemicals. A D–cell battery, for example, consists of a zinc container (the negative terminal) which surrounds a dark, moist mixture of manganese dioxide, powdered carbon, and ammonium chloride. A solid carbon rod runs through the center of the cell and serves as the positive terminal. A storage battery, such as the kind found in automobiles, has several cells. Each cell has lead electrodes immersed in a solution of sulfuric acid.

The chemicals found in most electric cells are quite common. In fact, you can easily build an electric cell yourself.

Procedure:

1. Prepare a strip of copper and a strip of zinc—the strips should be about 3.5 cm × 10 cm (1.5 in × 4 in)—by polishing with steel wool. Put the zinc strip in a glass or a beaker that contains 200 mL of a zinc nitrate solution. Put the copper strip in a glass or a beaker that contains 200 mL of a copper nitrate solution.

2. Using insulated wires with alligator clips, as shown in Figure 19, connect the zinc strip and copper strip to an ammeter (a device that measures electric current in amperes, or amps). Is there any current?

3. Next, connect the two solutions with a paper towel strip, as shown.

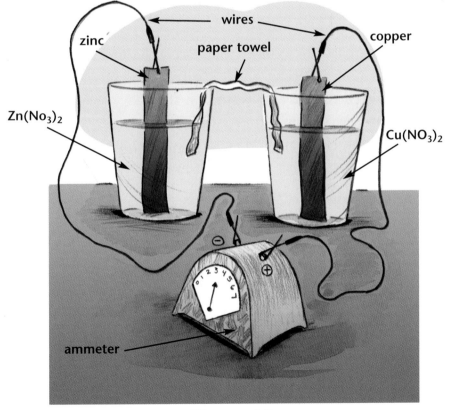

zinc

copper

wires

paper towel

$Zn(NO_3)_2$

$Cu(NO_3)_2$

ammeter

Figure 19.

This electric cell uses zinc and copper as electrodes. The electrodes are immersed in electrolytes (zinc nitrate and copper nitrate solutions).

Results and Conclusions

What happens when the two solutions diffuse along the towel and meet? If the ammeter needle moves below zero, reverse the wire that leads to the meter. Which metal is the positive electrode? Which metal is the negative electrode?

Remove the ammeter and replace it with a voltmeter (a device that measures energy per charge in volts). What is the voltage reading across this cell?

 Science Project Ideas

- For an electric cell to work, one electrode must provide electrons that will flow along a wire to the other electrode, where they are accepted. In the cell you built, which electrode provided electrons? Which electrode accepted the electrons? What is the overall chemical reaction that provides the energy in this cell?

- What is a Daniell cell? How does it work?

Appendix
SCIENCE SUPPLY COMPANIES

Carolina Biological Supply Company
2700 York Road
Burlington, NC 27215-3398
(800) 334-5551
http://www.carolina.com

Connecticut Valley Biological
   Supply Company
82 Valley Road
P.O. Box 326
Southampton, MA 01073
(800) 628-7748
http://www.ctvalleybio.com

Delta Education
80 Northwest Boulevard
P.O. Box 3000
Nashua, NH 03061-3000
(800) 258-1302
http://www.delta-education.com

Edmund Scientifics
60 Pearce Avenue
Tonawanda, NY 14150-6711
(800) 728-6999
http://scientificsonline.com

Educational Innovations, Inc.
362 Main Avenue
Norwalk, CT 06851
(888) 912-7474
http://www.teachersource.com

Fisher Science Education
4500 Turnberry Drive
Hanover Park, IL 60133
(800) 955-1177
http://www.fisheredu.com

Frey Scientific
80 Northwest Boulevard
Nashua, NH 03063
(800) 225-3739
http://www.freyscientific.com/

NASCO-Fort Atkinson
901 Janesville Avenue
P.O. Box 901
Fort Atkinson, WI 53538-0901
(800) 558-9595
http://www.nascofa.com/

NASCO-Modesto
4825 Stoddard Road
P.O. Box 3837
Modesto, CA 95352-3837
(800) 558-9595
http://www.eNasco.com

Sargent-Welch
P.O. Box 4130
Buffalo, NY 14217
(800) 727-4368
http://www.sargentwelch.com

Science Kit & Boreal Laboratories
777 East Park Drive
P.O. Box 5003
Tonawanda, NY 14151-5003
(800) 828-7777
http://sciencekit.com

Ward's Natural Science
P.O. Box 92912
Rochester, NY 14692-9012
(800) 962-2660
http://www.wardsci.com

Further Reading

Abbgy, Theodore S. *Elements and the Periodic Table*. Washington, D.C.: NSTA, 2001.

Fleisher, Paul, and Tim Seeley. *Matter and Energy: Principles of Matter and Thermodynamics*. New York: John Wiley and Sons, 2001.

Gardner, Robert. *Science Project Ideas About Kitchen Chemistry, Revised Edition*. Berkeley Heights, N.J.: Enslow Publishers, Inc., 2002.

_____. *Science Projects About Solids, Liquids, and Gases*. Berkeley Heights, N.J.: Enslow Publishers, Inc., 2000.

Kjelle, Marylou Morano. *Mixtures and Compounds*. New York: PowerKids Press, 2007.

Miller, Ron. *The Elements*. Minneapolis: Twenty-First Century Books, 2006.

Newmark, Ann. *Eyewitness Chemistry*. New York: DK Publishing, 2005.

Stwertka, Albert. *A Guide to the Elements*. New York: Oxford University Press, 2002.

Internet Addresses

American Chemistry Council, Inc. © 2007.
    <http://www.americanchemistry.com>

Chemistry for Kids
    <http://www.chem4kids.com>

Science Fair Ideas and News
    <http://www.sciencefaircenter.com/news>

The Science Fair Projects Depot: Science Project Ideas
    <http://www.sciencenerddepot.com>

Index